D0419790

THE BEST OF TV DINNERS

THE BEST OF

TV DINNERS

Hugh Fearnley-Whittingstall

CHANNEL 4 BOOKS

First published in 1999 by Channel 4 Books
an imprint of Macmillan Publishers Ltd
25 Eccleston Place London SW1W 9NF
and Basingstoke

Associated companies throughout the world

ISBN 0 7522 1354 7

Text copyright © Hugh Fearnley-Whittingstall 1999

All food photographs by Patrice de Villiers, Delicious Productions
Back cover photograph by Craig Easton
pine photograph by Nicky Johnstone

The right of Hugh Fearnley-Whittingstall to be identified as the
author of this work has been asserted by him in accordance
with the Copyright, Designs and Patents Act 1988.

All rights reserved. No part of this publication may be reproduced, stored
in or introduced into a retrieval system, or transmitted, in any form, or by
any means (electronic, mechanical, photocopying, recording or otherwise)
without the prior written permission of the publisher. Any person who does
any unauthorized act in relation to this publication may be liable to
criminal prosecution and civil claims for damages.

1 3 5 7 9 8 6 4 2

A CIP catalogue record for this book is available from the British Library.

Typeset by Blackjacks

Printed and bound by Mackays of Chatham Plc, Chatham, Kent

This book is sold subject to the condition that it shall not, by way of trade
or otherwise, be lent, re-sold, hired out, or otherwise circulated without the
publisher's prior consent in any form of binding or cover other than that in
which it is published and without a similar condition including this
condition being imposed on the subsequent purchaser.

This book accompanies the television series 'TV Dinners'
made by Ricochet Films for Channel 4.
Executive Producer: Nick Powell

Contents

Introduction

Almost exactly three years ago, shortly after my first TV series, 'A Cook on the Wild Side', aired on Channel 4, I received a telephone call. 'I have an idea for a new food series', said the voice at the other end, 'and I'd like to meet and talk to you about it.' 'Fine', I said, 'but can you give me the gist of it?' 'Well, basically, you just go and gatecrash other people's dinner parties.' I fixed a meeting and even as I put the phone down, I was thinking, 'I wish I'd thought of that.' A few days later, I was chatting to producer Nick Powell, of Ricochet films, in a West End coffee shop.

'TV Dinners' was a blissfully simple idea, which encapsulated what, in my mind, has been missing from so much of recent food-related television. In a word, conviviality. From its earliest days, television has had cookery programmes, and now more than ever home cooks are being bombarded with ideas and instructions from an ever expanding galaxy of 'star chefs'. I am not about to knock their talents or their influence – indeed, some of the home cooks from the four series are avid fans of the TV chefs – but how much more inspiring, it seemed to me, to find out what people actually choose to cook when their friends come round for dinner. And, by way of an added bonus, what they wear, how they lay the table, and what they talk about while they are eating. Most cooking shows finish dealing with a recipe at the point when it is put on a plate, ready to serve. In your average 'TV Dinners' story, that's just when things start to get *really* interesting.

After all, when you set about hosting a dinner party for friends, or indeed when you are invited to a dinner party at a friend's house, what is it that you most look forward to about the occasion? The dinner, or the party? The joy of 'TV Dinners' is that you can have both. We talk you through the dinner. . . and then we take you to the party.

Four series, seventy-six dinners and approximately 200,000 calories (that's only my personal tally) later, it's clear our optimism about the idea was well-founded. It's become equally clear, talking to fans of the show, that our audience find the people at the table at least as memorable as the food. We, and by extension our viewers, have enjoyed the hospitality of some remarkable characters. There was

Felicity Keebaugh, who set me, among other Herculean tasks, the challenge of containing her substantial and quivering bust inside a zebra-skin bustiere several sizes too small. There was Reg Gray, who misguidedly believes he is the reincarnation of Fred Astaire and, to his credit, takes every available opportunity to try and prove it. And there was Deborah Wilkins, who decided that the kindest thing to do with her beloved pet fish, who had outgrown his tank, was to put him on the barbecue.

Many of our home cooks brought an extraordinary degree of planning and control to the process of entertaining. Gordon Perrier, in the very first programme of the first series, was celebrating the arrival of a £20,000 table and chairs. He made eight different desserts for his guests, the colour of each coordinating with the plush velvet upholstery of the chairs. Michele Butterworth, celebrating 25 years in business as a hairdresser, embraced a theme not only of silver for the anniversary, but also of hair. Her guests, mainly other hairdressers, were required to style the sugar on their desserts as if they were a head of hair.

Other hosts were laid back to the point of horizontal. Paella specialist Dave Hayward didn't even start cooking until an hour after his guests arrived. Howard Morgan didn't know who was coming to his dinner, he just put the word out and waited to see who turned up. What all our cooks proved was that there is no sure-fire formula for successful entertaining, but rather that 'it takes all sorts'. Perhaps the only common ingredients are a passion for food and a penchant for good company. Besides that, anything goes. And believe me, on 'TV Dinners', some strange things often went!

But even the most eccentric and surprising characters were darned good cooks. There was hardly a dish I tasted that I didn't like and some of the food I tasted during the making of 'TV Dinners' ranks among the best I have eaten anywhere, ever. Thi Nguyen's Whelks stuffed with Minced Pork and her Summer Rolls made me feel like I'd actually been to Vietnam, Rose Billaud's Sweet and Sour Pork was a lip-sticking, finger-licking delight which surpasses anything I've had in a Chinese restaurant. George Dyer's Turbot Liver Pâté would justify international trade of its previously unsung principal ingredient. And Niamh Watmore's Amaretti Chocolate Torte would grace the table of any top flight restaurant, let alone a hastily assembled scout camp. I could go on...

In truth, what we found on our quest was not just an abundance of exciting home cooking, but confirmation that our food culture is in the throws of a revolution. The British home kitchen has become a hot-bed of creativity, from which we are gleaning inspiration and ideas from all over the world, to produce a heady mixture of dishes that are by turns original, classic, surprising, outrageous and in all cases, bursting with freshness and flavour. What you will find on these pages are clear instructions for the preparation of some of the very best dishes being cooked in Britain today. All the recipes have been tested by real home cooks in their own kitchens – if they can do it, so can you.

Making the four series has had many pleasures for me, not all of them connected directly with my stomach. I have travelled all over the country, got a bit of fishing in, and exercised my penchant for being a nosey parker in all kinds of interesting places. Without a doubt, however, the greatest pleasure has been to meet, share food, and talk about life with some 80-odd (some very odd) warm, talented, generous and genuinely hospitable hosts. On behalf of myself and everybody who has worked on all four series of 'TV Dinners', I would like to thank them all for having us.

HUGH FEARNLEY-WHITTINGSTALL
February 1999

starters

Canapés and Light Bites

Pepper Crostini

Just Like Mamma made – Nicky Samengo-Turner

serves eight

2 red peppers

2 yellow peppers

16 slices of white bread
or French loaf

3 cloves of garlic, halved

freshly ground black pepper

olive oil, to drizzle

16 fresh basil leaves, to garnish

1 Preheat the grill to hot. Slice the peppers in half and remove the stalk and seeds. Place on a grill pan, skin-side up and grill until the skin is blackened and bubbling. Once cooked, remove from the grill, put into a plastic bag and seal. As the peppers cool, the skins will be lifted off.

2 After about 15 minutes, remove from the bag and, with a sharp knife, pull the skin away from the pepper flesh. Slice the flesh into small strips.

3 If using sliced bread, cut out circles with a round pastry-cutter. Toast or fry the rounds of bread or slices of French loaf. Rub the slices of toast with the cut sides of the garlic to flavour them and then lay the strips of pepper on top, alternating the colours. Season with a little black pepper and a drizzle of olive oil.

4 Just before serving, warm under a hot grill and garnish with a fresh basil leaf.

Italian Flag

A Futurist Feast – Celia Lyttleton

This starter kicks off what was one of the most eccentric, memorable, and some would say, pretentious of all TV Dinners. The Futurists were, of course, passionately patriotic Italians, so it was only natural that Celia would want to fly the flag with this rather clever and tasty dish.

serves six

2 red peppers

1 tspn honey,
heated to make runny

small pinch of ground cinnamon

250 g/8 oz fresh spinach
leaves, thoroughly washed

1 tbspn olive oil

75 ml/3 fl oz crème fraîche

25 g/1 oz walnuts

pinch of grated nutmeg

1 large loaf of focaccia bread

300 g/10 oz mozzarella cheese

6 spring onions
or long carrot bâtons

1 Preheat the oven to 190°C/375°F/Gas mark 5.

2 To make the red stripe of the flag, place the whole red peppers on a baking tray. Glaze with honey and sprinkle with cinnamon. Bake for 25–35 minutes, until tender and lightly browned. Leave, covered, to cool. Remove the seeds and peel off the skin. Purée the flesh in a food processor or chop very finely with a knife.

3 To make the green stripe, wilt the spinach in olive oil over a medium heat, with a little water in the pan so that it doesn't burn. Purée in a food processor with the crème fraîche, walnuts and nutmeg. Or chop the spinach and walnuts finely with a knife or mezzaluna and mix with the crème fraîche and nutmeg.

4 Preheat the grill to high.

5 To make the white stripe, slice the focaccia bread into six rectangles. In the middle of each, place a slice of mozzarella cheese, leaving same-size patches on either side. Put under the preheated hot grill until melted, but do not let it brown.

6 To assemble the flag, spoon a stripe of pepper purée and a stripe of spinach purée on either side of the white cheese middle stripe, so that each piece of focaccia looks like the Italian flag. Make flag poles out of the spring onions or carrot bâtons.

7 Serve warm or at room temperature, but do not leave hanging around for long.

Tomato Bread with Spanish Ham

Valencian Paella Party – Dave Hayward

A simple Spanish way of flavouring bread is to rub it with a cut tomato and trickle over some olive oil. In this recipe, cured Spanish ham is used as a topping, but another variation would be to top the tomato-smeared bread with slices of piquant chorizo sausage and green olives.

serves eight, with other tapas

1 baguette

1–2 ripe tomatoes, halved

olive oil

salt

8 slices of cured Spanish ham (Serrano ham is the best)

1 Cut the baguette into thin slices.

2 Rub one side of each slice of bread with the cut side of the tomatoes.

3 Trickle a little olive oil over each slice of bread and season with salt.

4 Top each slice of bread with a piece of ham.

Anchovy and Black Olive Toasts

Valencian Paella Party – Dave Hayward

serves eight, with other tapas

1 baguette

1 clove of garlic, halved

olive oil

1 tin of anchovies, drained and mashed

approximately 30 black olives, halved and stoned

1 Preheat the oven to 180°C/350°F/Gas mark 4.
2 Cut the baguette into thin slices.
3 Rub the clove of garlic over each slice of bread and trickle over some olive oil.
4 Put the bread in the oven and toast until lightly golden and crisp.
5 Spread a little bit of anchovy on each toast and garnish with black olives.

Mozzarella in Carrozza

Just Like Mamma made – Nicky Samengo-Turner

serves eight

1 loaf of medium-sliced white bread

2 beef tomatoes

2 buffalo mozzarella cheeses

tin of anchovies, drained

bunch of fresh basil

dash of milk

4 eggs, beaten

salt and freshly ground black pepper

vegetable oil, for shallow-frying

1 Using a wine glass or tumbler, cut out twenty-four rounds of white bread.
2 Slice the tomatoes and mozzarella – the pieces need to be slightly smaller in size than the rounds of bread.
3 Make sandwiches using the bread, a piece of mozzarella, a slice of tomato, an anchovy and a couple of basil leaves. Press the sandwiches down firmly.
4 Mix the milk into the beaten eggs, season with salt and pepper and then dip the sandwiches into the egg mixture.
5 Heat the oil in a shallow frying-pan and fry the sandwiches until golden brown on both sides. Serve straight away.

Saltfish and Ackee Vol-au-vents

Caribbean Birthday Surprise – Trisha Wallace and Alison Haughton

The yellow, red and green of this dish make it a colourful as well as elegant canapé or starter. Ackee look a bit like scrambled eggs (they are also known as 'vegetable brains') and have a creamy texture. I'd never had them before, but was very taken with them. They are certainly worth seeking out in West Indian shops and ethnic grocers.

serves twelve as a canapé (two each), or six as starter (four each)

350 g/12 oz unsoaked saltfish, soaked overnight
2 tbspn sunflower oil
1 medium onion, chopped
½ red pepper, seeded and cut into 4 cm/1½ in long, thin slices
½ green pepper, seeded and cut into 4 cm/1½ in long, thin slices
2 fresh tomatoes, finely chopped
200 g/7 oz tin of chopped tomatoes
175 g/6 oz tinned ackee
24 small vol-au-vent cases
green part of 2 spring onions, finely chopped, to garnish

to prepare the saltfish

1 Drain the fish, transfer to a pan, cover with fresh water and bring to the boil. Drain again. Add more fresh, cold water and bring to the boil again. Repeat two or three times, tasting each time for saltiness. Leave to cool. Pick over fish, discarding any skin and bone.

to make the vol-au-vents

1 Heat the oil and fry the onion until soft.

2 Add the saltfish, the red and green peppers (keeping a few back for decoration) and fresh and tinned tomatoes. Cook until reduced to a thick sauce.

3 Drain any water from the tin of ackee, then stir into the tomato and pepper mixture until it is warmed through. Do not stir too vigorously as you don't want the ackee to break up.

4 Cook the vol-au-vent cases according to the packet instructions.

5 Reheat the sauce and fill the vol-au-vents. Garnish with chopped spring onions and slivers of red and green pepper. Serve hot or warm.

Pissaladière Canapés

Tory Blues – Marguerite Vincent

serves ten

For the flaky pastry

250 g/8 oz plain flour

pinch of salt

175 g/6 oz butter or margarine, frozen

iced water, to mix

For the pissaladière sauce

400 g/14 oz tin of peeled plum tomatoes

1 medium onion, roughly chopped

1 clove of garlic, roughly chopped

2 tspn sun-dried tomato paste

small bunch of fresh basil leaves

salt and freshly ground black pepper

2 tbspn olive oil

red and yellow cherry tomatoes, sliced, and black olives, to garnish

For the **faux** pesto topping

2 good handfuls of fresh basil leaves

25 g / 1 oz pumpkin seeds

2 tbspn olive oil

2 tbspn grated parmesan cheese

1 150 g/5 oz tub of crème fraîche

freshly ground black pepper

125 g/4 oz smoked salmon, cut into thin slices to garnish

1 To make the pastry, sift the flour and salt into a bowl and then grate the butter or margarine in, holding it in foil or paper. Mix with palette knife. Add just enough iced water to bind. Turn out on to a board, knead very lightly and then wrap in cling film and chill for half an hour. Then preheat the oven to 180°C/350°F/Gas mark 4.

2 Make the pissaladière sauce by puréeing all the ingredients, apart from the seasoning, olive oil and garnishes. Season to taste. Pour into a container, drizzle over the olive oil and microwave for 10 minutes. Set aside.

3 Make the *faux* pesto topping by processing the basil with the pumpkin seeds and olive oil, and then stirring in the parmesan and crème fraîche. Season to taste with pepper and set aside.

4 Roll out the pastry thinly, and stamp into circles 8 cm/3 in across. Place on two lightly greased baking trays and allow to rest for about 10 minutes.

5 Bake half the pastry circles for about 7 minutes and the rest for 15 minutes. Top the more lightly baked circles with the sauce and garnish with slices of red and yellow tomato and black olives. Return to the oven for another 7–10 minutes.

6 Spread the *faux* pesto on top of the fully baked pastry circles and then garnish with slices of smoked salmon.

Pâté Tartlets

Tea for the Girls – Enid Jean

serves twelve

for the pastry

250 g/8 oz plain flour

pinch of salt

150 g/5 oz butter, chilled

2 egg yolks

for the filling

redcurrant jelly

any smooth pâté (chicken liver is particularly good)

1 150 g/5 oz tub of cream cheese

1 heaped tspn mayonnaise

fresh redcurrants, to garnish

to make the pastry

1 Sift the flour and salt and rub in the butter. When the mixture resembles fine breadcrumbs, add the egg yolks and mix well with a round-bladed knife. Put the pastry in the fridge to chill for at least an hour.

2 Allow the pastry to return to room temperature. Preheat the oven to 160°C/325°F/Gas mark 3.

3 Roll the pastry out as thinly as possible and cut it into rounds that are big enough to fit the hollows in a small muffin tray or bun tray. Alternatively, press the pastry into the baking tray rather than rolling it, if it is very crumbly and hard to handle. Bake for 12–15 minutes in the middle of the oven. Allow to cool on a wire rack.

4 Spread the inside of the pastry shells with a thin layer of redcurrant jelly. Put enough pâté on top to fill the shells.

5 Mix the cream cheese with the mayonnaise to thin it. Put the mixture into a piping bag and carefully pipe a small amount of it on top of the pâté. Garnish with fresh redcurrants.

Soups

Mulligatawny Soup
Dinner with the Dawsons – Peggy Dawson

serves six

olive oil

butter

1 onion, chopped

1 stick of celery, finely chopped

1 large carrot, chopped

½ cooking apple, chopped

½ white of leek, chopped

small piece of fresh root ginger, peeled and finely chopped

375 g/12 oz lean shoulder of lamb, chopped

½ tspn ground cumin

½ tspn ground coriander

½ tspn ground turmeric

½ tspn ground cardamom

¼ tspn chilli powder

1 tbspn plain flour

1.2 litres/2 pints good stock

1 tbspn lemon juice

1 tbspn tomato purée

½ tspn sugar

salt and pepper

finely sliced leek, to garnish

1 Sweat the onion, celery and carrot together in a large, heavy-based saucepan, with a little olive oil and some butter for a few minutes. Add the cooking apple, leek and ginger and fry for a bit longer. Remove from the pan with a slotted spoon and set aside.

2 In the same pan, brown the lamb. Remove with a slotted spoon and set aside.

3 Fry the spices together briefly – make sure they don't burn. Add the flour, mix well, and cook for a minute. Then add the stock and stir in well. Add the lemon juice, tomato purée and sugar. Season to taste with salt and pepper.

4 Put all the cooked ingredients together in a pressure cooker and bring to the boil. Skim and then put the lid on and bring to 6.8 kg/15 lb pressure for 12 minutes. (If you are not using a pressure cooker, cook for about an hour and a half.)

5 Cool and reduce the pressure. Add more seasoning, if necessary. Skim off any surface fat. Purée three-quarters of the soup, then return to the pan and reheat all the soup slowly.

6 Serve with a few rings of finely sliced leek on top.

Chicken and Lemongrass Soup

Rumble in the Jungle – Felicity Keebaugh

As a hostess Felicity likes match-making and mischief-making and reckons that there are few better ways to excite your guests at the beginning of a meal than with the taste explosions of a spicy Thai-style soup. It does require a few specialist ingredients (such as Thai fish sauce and lemongrass) but, once you have these, they're extremely simple to use and very rewarding. Felicity uses little marzipan cutters to make her version of Thai sculpted vegetables to float in the aromatic broth.

serves six

1 free-range chicken,
1 kg/2¼ lb

1.5 litres/2½ pints water

2 each of leeks, carrots and onions (plus any other stock vegetables you fancy)

3 stalks of lemongrass

4 cm/1½ in piece of fresh root ginger, peeled and finely sliced

1–2 tbspn Thai fish sauce

1–2 tbspn groundnut oil

2 medium carrots, peeled

6 tinned water chestnuts

6 fresh mint leaves

18 fresh coriander leaves

1 red chilli, seeded and finely sliced diagonally

whites of 4 spring onions, finely sliced diagonally

1 Cut the breasts off the chicken and reserve.

2 Make a good chicken stock with the rest of the chicken carcass: add it to the water with the stock vegetables, bring everything to the boil, lower the heat and simmer very gently for at least 2 hours. Remove the carcass and vegetables and strain the stock through a sieve. *Optional:* To get a sparklingly clear soup, clarify the stock by adding the white and crushed shell of an egg to the stock when it is cool. Bring to the boil, whisking, and take off the heat. Strain through a sieve lined with muslin or a clean J-cloth. Repeat if necessary and you have the time.

3 Make 10 cm/4 in cuts down the lemongrass stalks, to release their heat and flavour. Simmer the lemongrass and the ginger in the stock for 20 minutes. Remove the lemongrass and ginger with a slotted spoon.

4 Add Thai fish sauce to taste, taking care that the broth does not become too salty.

5 Take the skin off the chicken breasts and cut the meat into thin strips. Stir-fry the chicken strips in a wok or non-stick pan in a little oil over a high heat, until nicely browned.

▶

6 Slice the carrots into very thin (2mm/⅛ in) discs and, using marzipan cutters or a knife, cut the discs into tiny shapes. Cut the water chestnuts into three thin slices and then into shapes. Alternatively, you could cut both vegetables into julienne strips.

7 Put into the simmering stock, with the chicken pieces, for just a minute before serving. The vegetables barely need to cook and should retain their crispness.

8 To serve, pour the soup into delicate Chinese soup bowls, making sure each serving has some vegetables and a few pieces of chicken. Finish each bowl with a single mint leaf, three coriander leaves, a few slices of chilli and some sliced spring onions.

Cream of Artichoke Soup
Colin and Duncan's Black Tie Dinner – Colin Beattie

serves eight

960 g/2 lb Jerusalem artichokes, peeled if wished

freshly-squeezed lemon juice

2 medium onions, sliced

30 g/1 oz butter

1 tbspn plain flour

1.25 litres/ 2 pints chicken stock

250 g/8 oz cream cheese

800 ml/½ pint milk

salt and pepper

extra-virgin olive oil or truffle oil, to garnish

1 Chop the artichokes and cover with water immediately, to prevent them from discolouring. Add a squeeze of lemon juice to the water to keep them white.

2 Fry the onion in the butter, with the drained artichokes, until the onion begins to soften.

3 Add the flour and cook briefly. Add the stock, a bit at a time, stirring to make a smooth sauce.

4 Bring to the boil and simmer for about 15 minutes, until the vegetables are soft.

5 Purée the soup and, if you left the artichoke skins on, sieve to remove them. Add the cream cheese and milk.

6 Reheat gently, without allowing it to boil, and season to taste with salt and pepper before serving hot. Drizzle a little olive oil or, for extra luxury, truffle oil, on each serving, to garnish.

Minestrone Madras with Spicy Bruschetta

Old Girls' Reunion – Heather Matuozzo

serves four

for the soup

2 cloves of garlic, crushed

3 tspn Madras curry paste

1 large onion, diced

2 carrots, diced

2 potatoes, diced

1 courgette, diced

4 tbspn olive oil

600 ml/1 pint vegetable stock

(2 x) 400 g/14 oz tin of plum tomatoes

120 g/4 oz green lentils

250 g/8 oz green or white cabbage, shredded

250 g/8 oz tin of cannellini beans, drained

3 tspn tomato purée

250 g/8 oz macaroni

salt and pepper

for the bruschetta

bloomer loaf or similar, thickly sliced

5 tbspn olive oil

6 garlic cloves, smashed

cumin seeds

finely chopped fresh coriander, to garnish

to make the soup

1 In a large, heavy-bottomed pan, fry the garlic, Madras paste and diced vegetables in olive oil, until browned. Add the stock, tomatoes, lentils and cabbage. Bring to the boil and then turn the heat down to a simmer. Cook until the lentils are almost tender, about 40 minutes.

2 Add the beans and tomato purée. Stir, add the pasta, season and continue cooking until the pasta is *al dente*, about 10 minutes. Season with salt and pepper.

to make the bruschetta

1 Meanwhile, preheat the oven to 200°C/ 400°F/Gas mark 6. Grease a baking tray and put the bread slices on it.

2 In a thick-based pan, heat the olive oil. Add the garlic and fry it, to flavour the oil. Scoop out the garlic.

3 Spoon the oil on to the bread, sprinkle with cumin seeds and bake until golden brown. Serve the bruschetta with a light sprinkling of finely chopped coriander.

Corn, Chilli and Cheese Soup

Scouts Honour – Niamh Watmore

serves six

2 tbspn butter

1 onion, finely chopped

450 g/15 oz sweetcorn kernels

2 litres/3½ pints stock

1 tspn salt

1 green pepper, seeded and finely diced

2 green chillies, seeded and chopped

3 tomatoes, peeled and diced

salt and pepper

150 g/5 oz Cheddar cheese, grated, to serve

snipped fresh chives, to garnish

1 Heat 1 tbspn of the butter, add the onion and sweat until soft.

2 Add the sweetcorn, stock and salt, bring to the boil and simmer for 15 minutes.

3 Purée half the soup. Return the puréed half to the pan with the remaining soup.

4 Briefly sauté the green pepper and chillies in the remaining butter. Add the tomatoes; season and cook for 2 minutes.

5 Add to the corn soup. Check the seasoning.

6 To serve, divide the cheese and chives between six bowls and ladle the soup on top.

Crab, Coconut and Coriander Soup

Cornish Fish Barbecue – Clare Montcrieff-Hunt

serves six

for the stock

500–900 g/1–2 lb whole
pollock or cod, coley or other
inexpensive white fish fillets

1 whole medium-size crab,
cut into bits

2 medium onions

bunch of fresh coriander,
chopped

4 stalks of lemongrass, sliced

6 cloves of garlic

1.75 litres/3 pints water

salt and pepper

for the soup

butter

olive oil

1 large onion, chopped

3 cloves of garlic, crushed

2 medium potatoes,
peeled and chopped

bunch of fresh coriander,
finely chopped

2 tbspn home-made (recipe
follows) or commercial piri-piri
sauce or other chilli sauce

500 g/1 lb fresh
mixed crabmeat

1 whole crab

600 ml/1 pint coconut milk

salt and pepper

to make the stock

1 Place all the ingredients in a large saucepan.
Bring to the boil and allow to simmer for
about an hour.

2 Strain and set aside until needed.

to make the soup

1 Melt a knob of butter and a dash of olive
oil in a large saucepan. Add the onion, garlic
and potatoes. Soften over a gentle heat for
5 minutes.

2 Add the stock, coriander and piri-piri sauce
(see overleaf) and season to taste. Simmer for
20 minutes.

3 Mash well to break up the potatoes. Add the
crabmeat and the meat from the body and claws
of the whole crab. You can also put in the small
crab claws for decoration. Simmer for 5 minutes
and then add the coconut milk. Stir well and
serve at once.

▶

for the piri-piri sauce

300 ml/½ pint olive oil

juice of ½ lemon

10 red bird's eye chillies, seeded and finely chopped (or similar)

10 cloves of garlic, crushed

1 jalapeño pepper, seeded and finely chopped

2 tbspn Madroño (distilled orange blossom) or preferred alcoholic spirit

dash of balsamic vinegar

4 small, long, fresh red chillies, to decorate

handful of chopped fresh coriander

salt and pepper, to taste

cayenne pepper, to taste

to make the piri-piri sauce

1 Combine all the ingredients in a screw-top jar. Seal the lid tightly, shake well and then leave for a week, to marinate.

2 The sauce will be ready to use after a week and can be stored in a cool place for up to 12 months.

Note: If planning to make your own piri-piri sauce for this recipe, remember it needs to be prepared a week in advance.

Chicken Soup with Kneidlich and Lockshen

A Kosher Celebration – Lindsey Jacobs

serves ten

2 kg/4 lb boiling fowl, including giblets, feet, neck and rear end if possible (about 750 g/1½ lb if oven-ready)

3 onions, halved, skins left on (to give a better colour to the soup)

6 large carrots, sliced

4 sticks of celery, chopped

2 parsnips, sliced

large bunch of fresh parsley

for the kneidlich

makes 24

275 g/9 oz medium matso meal

1 tspn ground mixed spice

1 cup (equal to the volume of matso meal) boiling water

1 egg

1 tbspn chicken fat (optional, but makes them lighter)

salt and pepper

for the lockshen

300 g/110 oz egg vermicelli

to make the soup

1 Put all the ingredients in a pan, cover with water, bring rapidly to the boil and skim with a slotted spoon. Turn down the heat, cover and simmer gently for 6 hours. Leave to cool.

2 Throw away the onion, parsley, parsnips, and celery. Strain the rest, skin the chicken, remove the bones and put all the meat back in the pan. Chill overnight.

3 Remove any fat from the top with a spoon, and reserve (this is known as 'shmaltz'). Skim any remaining bits with a tea strainer. Boil up and add kneidlich and lockshen.

to make the kneidlich

1 Mix everything together with wet hands and roll bits of the mixture into balls. Put in the fridge to cool and then add to the boiling soup. Simmer for 10 minutes.

to make the lockshen

1 Boil the egg vermicelli for 2 minutes. Add to the soup, or divide between individual serving bowls and ladle the soup on top.

Nettle Soup

A Jamaican Farewell – Paige Mulroy

To say farewell to her Irish friends, Paige wanted to serve up something wild from Irish soil – nettles fitted the bill perfectly. Pick only the youngest stinging nettles, avoiding any that have gone to seed, and use only the top crown of leaves.

serves six

colander-full of nettles, washed
and picked over, trimmed of
thick stalks and roughly chopped

olive oil

1 onion, finely chopped

4 cloves of garlic, finely sliced

1 tomato

1.5 litres/2½ pints filtered water

1 'scotch bonnett' pepper,
seeded and finely chopped

salt and pepper

1 Carefully wash the nettles and remove the leaves from the stalks.

2 Heat the oil in a large saucepan and sauté the onion, garlic and tomato for a few minutes, until slightly softened.

3 Shake the water off the nettles and add them to the pan; toss in the oil, to seal in the flavour.

4 Add the water, salt and chopped 'Scotch Bonnet' pepper.

5 Bring to the boil and allow to simmer for about 10 minutes. Season to taste and serve hot.

Fish

Sushi Rolls

All over the Pacific – Penny Sinclair

You can buy the special nori seaweed and wasabi, the zesty Japanese horseradish mustard, in good oriental grocers and some supermarkets.

makes twenty-four pieces of sushi, to serve six

500 g/1 lb/4 x 150 ml cups Thai fragrant rice or sushi rice

1 litre/1¾ pints/4 x 150 ml cups water

120 ml/4 fl oz/½ 150 ml cup rice vinegar

6 sheets of nori Seaweed

thinly sliced spring onion

250 g/8 oz fresh fish, e.g. halibut, tuna, scallops or salmon, cut into 3 cm/1½ in slices

wasabi

to serve

pickled root ginger

wasabi

1 Put the rice and water in a pan and cook until all the water is absorbed. Let stand for 10 minutes. Add the rice vinegar and stir in.

2 Toast the individual sheets of seaweed lightly over a gas flame, being careful not to let them catch fire.

3 Place the seaweed on a sushi mat. Spoon on some rice and then, with wet fingers, flatten the rice out to the edges, leaving 3 cm/1½ in of the seaweed at the top and 1 cm/½ in at the bottom.

4 Put some thinly sliced spring onion at the bottom end of the rice, then some fish lightly coated with wasabi.

5 Very carefully fold over the edge of the seaweed and, using the sushi mat, carefully roll the seaweed and rice up.

6 When you get to the end put a little water on the edge and roll up. Squeeze the sushi roll firmly to make sure that the seaweed has stuck. Repeat with the remaining sheets of seaweed and filling.

7 Wet the knife and cut each roll into four pieces. Serve with pickled root ginger and wasabi.

Taramasalata

Greco-Italian Surprise Party – Marina Schofield

*Use a light olive oil for this as there shouldn't be an overpoweringly
strong taste of olives in the finished dish.*

serves twenty

1 large loaf of stale unsliced
white bread (3 days old)

150 g/5 oz smoked cod's roe

1 lemon

175–200 ml/6–7 fl oz olive oil
(not virgin)

salt

to serve

pitta bread and/or crudités

1 Soak the whole loaf, with the crust on, in a bowl
of water for 5 minutes. Take out of the water, rip
in half, scoop out the innards of loaf, discarding
the crust. Squeeze out all the water from the
remaining bread.

2 Put the cod's roe and lemon juice together in a
food processor. Add a little bread to the roe
mixture, along with a little of the oil, and process
thoroughly. Repeat until all the bread and oil
are used, or until the mixture has the required soft
consistency. Add salt to taste.

3 Serve warm with pitta bread and/or crudités,
to dip in.

Turbot Liver Pâté

Trawlerman's Supper – George Dyer

*Although Turbot livers are not easily available, I wanted to include this
recipe because it is so very delicious. If you have a good and friendly
fishmonger, or indeed know a trawlerman, ask him to save you some.*

serves six

2 tbspn olive oil

1 Spanish onion, roughly
chopped

120 g/4 oz mushrooms,
quartered

4 rashers of streaky bacon,
chopped

5 cloves of garlic, roughly
chopped

300 ml/½ pint dry sherry

4–6 turbot livers

1 Preheat the oven to 150°C/300°F/Gas mark 3.
Heat the oil in a deep saucepan. Add the
onion, mushrooms, bacon and garlic.

2 Add the dry sherry and turbot livers and fry until
the livers are golden. Remove from the heat.

3 Purée the mixture until smooth and then pour into
a terrine dish or small loaf tin. Cover with foil.

4 Pour a little water into an ovenproof dish.
Place the clay pot or loaf tin in this and bake for
1½ hours.

5 Remove from the roasting dish and leave to go
cold. Turn out of the cooking container and serve
with warm crusty bread or wholemeal toast.

Quails' Eggs in Smoked Salmon Nests with Lime Mayonnaise

Gourmet Night – Gordon Irvine

A very easy starter, which looks special and is made a little unusual by the lime mayonnaise. You could flavour a good ready-made mayonnaise with lime juice and zest if you do not want to make your own from scratch. When making home-made mayonnaise, all the ingredients should be at room temperature. If the egg or the oil is cold, the mayonnaise tends to separate. This lime mayonnaise is also delicious with any hot or cold poached fish, especially salmon and sea bass.

serves six

12 fresh quails' eggs

175 g/6 oz smoked salmon, cut in strips 6 mm/¼ in wide and 8 cm/3 in long

for the lime mayonnaise

1 egg yolk

150 ml/¼ pint oil, half olive, half sunflower or groundnut

juice of ½ lime

thinly grated zest of 1 lime

salt and freshly ground black pepper

1 Put the eggs into a pan of boiling water and cook for 3 minutes. Drain and run under cold water to stop them from cooking any more.

2 To peel, roll the eggs firmly but gently on the work surface to crack the shell all over. This makes them much easier to peel.

to make the lime mayonnaise

1 Place the egg yolk in a mixing bowl and whisk with a balloon whisk (or an electric or manual hand whisk).

2 Mix in the oil very slowly, adding a very small trickle to start off with and slightly more as it thickens, whisking all the time.

3 Gradually whisk in the lime juice and half the lime zest.

4 Season with salt and pepper to taste. Add more lime zest if desired.

5 Cover the mayonnaise and store in the fridge until ready to use.

▶

to serve

1 On a large white plate, arrange the smoked salmon strips into 12 small circular shapes, building them up in layers to make 12 nests, each one big enough to support one quail's egg.

2 Place a peeled quail's egg in the centre of each nest.

3 Spoon the mayonnaise over the quails' eggs and smoked salmon nests. Do this at the last minute so that it does not run or get a skin on it.

Puff Pastries with Anchovy Ice Cream

Keeping up Appearances – June Ainsworth

serves eight

2 egg yolks

60 g/2½ oz cream cheese

120 ml/4 fl oz double cream, lightly whipped

25 g/1 oz tinned anchovy fillets, drained and chopped

pinch of cayenne pepper

2 tbspn chopped fresh parsley

120 g/4 oz puff pastry

1 dspn porridge oats

1 Lightly whisk one egg yolk, until creamy. Whisk in the cream cheese and then fold in the whipped cream, anchovies, cayenne pepper and parsley. Transfer to a shallow container and freeze for about 2 hours, or until hard.

2 On a lightly floured surface, roll out the pastry 3 mm/⅛ in thick. Using an 8 cm/3 in cutter, cut out eight circles and transfer to a dampened baking tray. Take a small knife and raise the edges slightly to encourage rising. Chill for 30 minutes. Preheat the oven to 220°C/425°F/Gas mark 7.

3 Brush the pastry circles with the remaining beaten egg yolk and then sprinkle porridge oats over them. Bake for 7–10 minutes or until the pastry is golden brown and the oats are toasted.

4 Remove the pastries from the oven and split in half. Spoon some of the anchovy ice cream into each one and serve.

Lobster Pâté with Rosé Sauce

The West Essex Gourmet's Reunion – Ron Heath

serves eight

for the pâté

375 g/12 oz tinned cooked lobster meat

175 g/6 oz full-fat cream cheese

2 tbspn orange lumpfish roe

3 hard-boiled egg yolks

3 tbspn dry vermouth

salt and pepper

300 ml/½ pint double cream

2 tbspn water

3 rounded tspn powdered gelatine

2 tbspn chopped fresh chives

8 small cooked asparagus spears (fresh or tinned)

for the sauce

300 ml/½ pint rosé wine

1 small shallot, finely chopped

1 level tbspn chopped fresh dill

300 ml/½ pint soured cream

3 tbspn orange lumpfish roe

2 hard-boiled egg yolks, sieved

to garnish

8 small cooked asparagus spears (fresh or tinned)

finely diced cucumber

to make the pâté

1 Put the lobster into a liquidizer, with the cream cheese, lumpfish roe, egg yolks and vermouth, and blend until smooth. Pour the mixture into a bowl, add salt and pepper to taste and stir in the double cream, until evenly blended.

2 Put the water in a small bowl and sprinkle in the gelatine. Stand the bowl in a pan of hot water and stir until the gelatine has dissolved. Stir into the lobster mixture and then leave on one side until it starts to thicken. Fold in the chives.

3 Lightly grease a 1.2-litre/2-pint loaf tin. Spoon half the mixture in and then lay the asparagus spears, whole or cut into shorter lengths, on top. Spread the remaining mixture evenly over the asparagus. Chill in the refrigerator for 3–4 hours, or until set.

to make the sauce

1 Put the rosé wine, shallot and dill in a small pan. Bring to the boil and simmer until the wine has reduced to about 2 tbspn. Strain the wine and then leave to cool.

2 Mix the wine with the soured cream, lumpfish and sieved egg yolks. Chill in the refrigerator until needed. (Do not blend the sauce in a liquidizer – this will make it too thin.)

to serve

1 Dip the loaf tin briefly in hot water and turn the pâté out on to a dish. Cut it into eight slices and lay each slice on a plate. Trickle over a little of the pink sauce and garnish with the asparagus spears and diced cucumber. Serve the remaining sauce separately, in a small jug.

Cockles and Laverbread

The Feast of Samhain – Ozi Osmond

The traditional Celtic feast of Samhain is, apparently, a kind of Harvest Festival-cum-Halloween with marauding spirits and young wenches suddenly getting pregnant... or so Ozi told us with credible Welsh relish. Whatever the vagaries of the occasion, Ozi and his wife Hilary were great hosts, both to their own guests and to my crew.

serves six

750 g/1½ lb oats

375 g/12 oz laverbread

olive oil, for frying

approximately 5 litres/8 pints medium-size cockles in the shell

3–4 tbspn water

3–4 tbspn white wine

50 g/2 oz butter, plus extra for frying

1 clove of garlic, crushed

pepper

6 slices of lemon, to serve

1 Take a handful of oats and enough laverbread to bind the oats together and shape into a ball. Flatten out to make a cake about 8 cm/3 in in diameter and 5 mm/¼ in thick. Repeat with the remaining laverbread and oats. You need one cake per person.

2 Heat some olive oil in a frying-pan. Lightly fry the laverbread cakes for a couple of minutes on each side. Keep warm while you cook the cockles.

3 Steam open the cockles in the water with the white wine and butter, in a covered pan, for about 3 minutes. Discard any that have not opened by then. Remove the cockles from the shells.

4 Strain the cooking juices and reduce them by two-thirds.

5 Heat a little more oil and a knob of butter in a pan and sauté the crushed garlic. Add the cockles and reduced juices and lightly cook them for a couple of minutes in the garlicky butter and oil. Make sure that you don't cook the cockles for too long otherwise they will be very tough. Check the seasoning: the cockles are very salty so you shouldn't need any more salt but add pepper to taste.

6 Serve with the laverbread and a slice of lemon.

Seafood Fishcakes with Garlic and Chilli Sauce

Trawlerman's Supper – George Dyer

Prepared in the ship's galley, these were the most extravagant fish cakes I've ever seen – but if you've got it on board, flaunt it!

serves eight

12 shell-on scallops
1 small live lobster
2 cod fillets, about 500 g/1 lb or a whole cod
2 monkfish fillets, about 500 g/1 lb
2.25 kg/5 lb potatoes
plain flour, seasoned for coating
oil for shallow-frying
2 live crabs

for the sauce

12 good-sized tomatoes
2 tbspn olive oil
1 onion, finely chopped
4 red chillies, seeded, if wished, and finely chopped
8 cloves of garlic, finely chopped
1 yellow pepper, finely chopped
400 g/14 oz tin of plum tomatoes
sun-dried tomato paste

to prepare the fish

1 Take the scallops out of their shells and wash in cold water. Chop in half, if they are large.

2 Place the lobster's head in a pot of boiling water and then slowly drop the rest of the body into the water. Boil for 20 minutes. Allow half an hour to cool. Break off the claws and the head; bend the tail right over and squeeze in your hands, to get the meat out.

3 To kill a crab, stick a knife in his underbelly in between his feelers. Repeat with the other crab. Boil in salted water for 20 minutes. Leave to cool (George places it on deck, through the roof). When it is cold, pop the mouth piece out and set aside the brown meat. Pop out the 'purse' (the underbelly) with your thumbs and remove the white meat.

4 If you are using cod you've caught yourself, run a knife underneath the belly of the fish and remove the guts. With a knife, run it backwards along the fish to remove the scales. Cut off the head and tail.

5 If the monkfish has not been skinned, place in a pot of boiled water, for a few minutes, until the skin begins to form a jelly. Remove from the water – this should make it very easy to remove the skin.

▶

to make the fish cakes

1 Place the cod fillets, monkfish and scallops in a pan, with a little water. Steam for 10–15 minutes. Drain in a colander and allow to go cold.

2 Boil the potatoes until soft.

3 Meanwhile, remove the lobster meat and crab meat from the shells.

4 When the potatoes are cooked, drain, cover with a clean tea towel and place in a cool, breezy area for around 20 minutes, until cool (again, George makes use of the deck for this).

5 Place two-thirds of the potatoes in another bowl and mash them. Add all the seafood.

6 Press into fishcake shapes in your hands and then toss in flour.

7 Heat the oil and shallow-fry the cakes, taking care not to move them around too much as they are fragile.

8 Once golden brown, place on kitchen roll, to remove the oil, and transfer to a warm oven (150°C/300°F/Gas mark 3), to keep warm while you cook the sauce.

to make the sauce

1 Place the tomatoes in boiling water for a minute or so and then remove their skins. Allow to cool and then roughly chop them.

2 Heat the oil in a heavy-based frying pan and fry the onions and chillies, until soft. Add the garlic and yellow pepper, the canned and fresh tomatoes and the tomato paste. Stir well.

3 Remove from the heat and purée until fine. Serve with the fishcakes.

Saucy Spratlings with a Spicy Split-pea Sauce

Trafalgar Night Fever – Holly Waghorn

serves twelve

48 sprats

120 g/4 oz plain flour

3 tspn ground turmeric

salt and pepper

vegetable oil, for shallow-frying

for the sauce

250 g/8 oz split peas, soaked overnight

salt

1 tspn ground turmeric

to garnish

slices of lime

watercress

to make the spicy split-pea sauce

1 Cook the split peas in water to cover, with a little salt and the turmeric, for 30 minutes. Mash the split peas to make a thick sauce. Keep warm while you cook the sprats.

to make the spicy spratlings

1 Remove the heads and tails of each sprat. Slice down the belly of the fish, open and remove the guts and backbone. Rinse each fish in salty water.

2 Mix the flour, turmeric, salt and pepper together. Dip each fish in and lightly coat with the mixture.

3 Heat the oil in a frying-pan and shallow fry each of the fish, making sure that both sides are cooked, until golden brown. Pat dry on some kitchen paper, to absorb excess oil.

4 Serve the sprats on a plate, with the split-pea sauce and garnished with some slices of lime and a little watercress. Serve with some plain boiled rice.

Koulibiac

Welcome to the World – Sue O' Neil

for the filling

serves fifteen

50 g/2 oz butter

1 large onion, chopped

250 g/8 oz mushrooms,
finely chopped

250 g/8 oz long-grain white
rice, boiled, drained and cooled

50 g/2 oz flaked almonds,
lightly toasted

500 g/1 lb smoked haddock,
cooked and flaked

1 tspn finely chopped preserved
ginger

1 tbspn chopped raisins

1 tbspn lemon juice

salt and pepper

375 g/12 oz frozen
puff pastry, thawed

1 egg, beaten, to glaze

for the sauce

butter or oil for frying

2 shallots, finely chopped

300 ml/½ pint single cream

150 ml/¼ pint fish
or chicken stock

1 tbspn finely chopped
fresh herbs, e.g. parsley,
chives or thyme

1 tspn prepared French mustard

squeeze of lemon juice

salt and freshly ground
black pepper

to make the filling

1 Preheat the oven to 220°C/450°F/Gas mark 7.
Melt the butter in a saucepan. Add the onion
and cook until soft, then add the mushrooms and
cook until they are soft. Increase the heat briefly,
to evaporate the liquid.

2 Put into a mixing bowl, with the rice, almonds,
haddock, ginger, raisins and lemon juice. Mix
together well, and season to taste. Set aside
to cool.

to assemble the Koulibiac

1 Roll out the pastry thinly and cut into squares.

2 Put a spoonful of filling into the centre of each
pastry square and enclose, by sticking opposite
corners of the square together with a little water
and sealing the edges, to form little 'pyramid'
shapes. Brush with beaten egg.

3 Bake for approximately 25 minutes, or until the
pastry is brown and the filling is cooked.

to make the sauce

1 Make the sauce by lightly frying the shallots in a
knob of butter or a little oil; set aside. Boil the
cream with the fish stock for 5 minutes, until
thickened, and then stir in the remaining
ingredients, including the shallot, seasoning
to taste.

2 Serve in a separate dish, with the koulibiac
parcels. The parcels can be eaten either hot
or cold.

Gravadlax with Dill and Mustard Mayonnaise

In Search of Love – Simon Kelton

serves eight

1.5 kg/3½ lb wild brown trout, filleted
_____
2 tbspn olive oil
_____
3 tbspn ground white peppercorns
_____
50 g/2 oz brown sugar
_____
120 g/4 oz sea salt
_____
250 g/8 oz chopped fresh dill
_____
2 tspn brandy

for the mayonnaise (makes 90 ml/3 fl oz)

1 tbspn white-wine vinegar
_____
1 tbspn Dijon mustard
_____
1 tbspn chopped fresh dill
_____
2 tspn sugar
_____
salt and pepper
_____
4 tbspn of olive oil

to serve

4 avocados, peeled and sliced
_____
juice of 1 lemon or lime
_____
4 papayas, peeled and sliced

1 Smear the fillets with olive oil. Sprinkle with peppercorns.
2 Mix the sugar, salt and dill together. Divide the mixture into three. Cover each fillet with a third of the mixture. Sprinkle the brandy on to each fillet.
3 Sandwich the fillets together and cover with the remainder of the mixture. Wrap the fillets together in tin foil and weigh down with a very heavy object. Leave to marinate at room temperature for at least 24 hours.
4 Place in the fridge for the final 4 hours before serving.

to make the mayonnaise

1 Have all the ingredients at room temperature. Combine all the ingredients in a bowl, except the oil. Add the oil drop by drop, while blending or whisking vigorously. Add it slightly more quickly as the mayonnaise thickens. Place the finished sauce in the fridge to chill.

to serve

1 Peel and slice the avocados and toss the slices in citrus juice to prevent discolouration. Halve the papayas and scoop out the flesh with a melon baller.
2 To serve, scrape off the dill coating. Place the fillets on a board and cut into thin vertical slices. Fold the slices into small piles on each plate. Serve with slices of avocado, papaya balls and mayonnaise.

Highland Pibroch

The Laird's Supper – Michael Dudgeon

I've no idea what a 'Pibroch' is, or was, but these are quite clearly fish sausages and very tasty they are too.

serves ten–twelve

for the 'sausages'

500 g/1 lb smoked haddock
500 g/1 lb fresh haddock
2 egg whites
150 ml/¼ pint double cream
500 g/1 lb smoked trout, flaked
500 g/1 lb, peeled, cooked prawns, chopped
sea salt and freshly ground black pepper

for the sauce

2 onions, very finely chopped
butter, for frying
450 ml/¾ pint fish stock
pinch of saffron
250 ml/8 fl oz white wine
450 ml/¾ pint single cream

to garnish

10–12 langoustines, cooked, to decorate
10–12 sprigs of fresh flat-leaf parsley

to make the 'sausages'

1 Process the smoked and fresh haddock, egg whites and cream together.

2 Fold the trout and prawns into the mixture (avoid breaking up the fish too much).

3 Season and form into about 20–24 'sausages', about 8 cm/3 in long, and wrap in plenty of cling film, like little Christmas crackers.

4 Poach for approximately 10 minutes in a shallow pan of water. Have ready a bowl of iced water and drop the cooked sausages in for a minute, so that the cling film can be easily removed. Put into a warmed dish and keep warm in the oven.

to make the sauce

1 Fry the onions in the butter. Add the stock and saffron. When the stock has reduced to the required consistency, add the white wine and then the cream and boil vigorously.

2 To serve, place two fish sausages on each plate, pour over some sauce and garnish with a langoustine and a sprig of parsley.

Meat, Poultry and Game

Stuffed Vine Leaves
Eastern Promise – Liz Kabbara

serves twelve

500 g/1 lb minced lamb

500 g/1 lb long-grain rice

50 g/2 oz butter

1 tspn each ground cinnamon, nutmeg and mixed spice, and ½ tspn ground allspice, mixed together

salt

4 x 250 g/8 oz packets of prepared vine leaves

750 g/1½ lb boneless breast or leg of lamb, cut in chunks or slices

2 tbspn olive oil

4–6 cloves

2 cloves of garlic, chopped

2 tbspn chopped fresh mint

juice of 2 lemons

1 Mix together the minced lamb, rice, butter and half the spice mixture; season with salt.

2 Separate the vine leaves. Put ½ tspn of the stuffing mixture in the centre of the leaf. Tuck the sides in and roll up into a tight, neat cylinder, about the size of your little finger. Set aside.

3 Fry the breast or fillet of lamb chunks or slices quickly in the oil, until browned. Season with salt and the remaining spice mixture and place in the bottom of a large, flameproof dish.

4 Pack the stuffed leaves neatly into the dish, on top of the lamb. Sprinkle on the cloves, garlic and mint. Weight the rolls down with a dinner plate topped with a heavy weight. Add two glasses of water. Bring to the boil and then turn the heat down as low as possible and leave for 2–3 hours (adding more water occasionally, if necessary).

5 Remove the plate, add the lemon juice and cook for a further hour. Taste and add salt, if necessary.

Black Pudding Wontons with Balsamic Sauce

Leaving Liverpool – Jon Ashton

A very cheeky dish from a very cheeky and likeable young cook.

serves four

for the wontons

1–2 tbspn oil

2 shallots, finely chopped

3 spring onions, finely chopped

2 cloves of garlic, finely chopped

small piece of fresh root ginger, finely chopped

1 stalk of lemongrass – finely chopped

120 g/4 oz black pudding, finely chopped

250 g/8 oz minced chicken or pork

salt and pepper

handful of fresh chives, finely chopped

1 packet frozen wonton wrappers, thawed but kept chilled

1 egg, beaten

oil, for deep-frying

for the sauce

300 ml/½ pint balsamic vinegar

to make the wontons

1 Heat the oil in a large frying-pan and gently fry the shallots, spring onions, garlic, ginger and lemongrass. Add the black pudding to the mixture and continue to fry gently for a minute.

2 Take off the heat and, in a large bowl, mix with the minced chicken or pork. Season well with salt and pepper.

3 Stir in the chives. Lay out the wonton wrappers. Brush egg along two sides of each wrapper. Place a tablespoon of the mixture in the centre of each wonton sheet and pinch the edges together, to seal.

4 Heat the oil until very hot. Deep-fry the wontons, in batches if necessary, for 2–3 minutes or until golden brown. Drain on kitchen paper and keep them hot. Serve as soon as possible, with the balsamic sauce drizzled on top.

to make the reduced balsamic sauce

1 Pour the balsamic vinegar into a pan, bring to the boil and reduce to a thick, sticky mixture (this produces an eye-stinging vapour, so keep the doors shut and don't get your nose too close!). Drizzle over each wonton.

Pigeon Pâté with Flowerpot Bread

Run Rabbit Run – Hilary Waterhouse

serves ten

75 g/3 oz butter

2 tbspn olive oil

2 large onions, chopped

1 large clove of garlic, chopped

500 g/1 lb chicken livers

4 bay leaves

4 red peppercorns

750 g/1½ lb unsmoked streaky bacon rashers, rinded

8 pigeon breasts

1 egg, lightly beaten

1 tbspn redcurrant jelly

salt and pepper

25 g/1 oz pistachio nuts, sliced

1 Preheat the oven to 180°C/350°F/Gas mark 4. Lightly grease two 1 kg/2 lb loaf tins.

2 Heat 50 g/2 oz of butter and the oil in a frying-pan, add the chopped onions and garlic and fry until golden brown. Add the chicken livers and fry until they are cooked. Set aside to cool.

3 Take the loaf tins and place the bay leaves in a line at the bottom of each one. Place the red peppercorns in a diamond shape in the centre of each line. Stretch the bacon rashers with the back of a knife. Then line each of the tins with the rashers of bacon, leaving enough bacon hanging over the side of the tin to cover the top of the mixture.

4 Slice the pigeon breasts lengthways. In a frying-pan, melt the remaining butter, add the pigeon and fry gently till lightly browned.

5 Purée the cooled chicken-liver mixture, with the egg, redcurrant jelly and salt and pepper to taste.

6 Spread a layer of the blended mixture over the bacon. Then add a layer of pigeon breasts, sprinkled with sliced pistachios. Repeat the chicken-liver and pigeon-breast layers until they near the top of the tin, making sure a chicken-liver mixture layer is last. Fold the bacon over the top and patch up the middle with more bacon, if needed.

7 Place the tins in a bain-marie (a roasting tin filled with hot water to about halfway up the sides of the loaf tins). Bake at the top of the oven for 1½ hours. Leave to cool in the tins.

8 When completely cool, run a knife between the loaf tins and the pâté to ease it out and invert the tins to turn out the pâté. Serve in slices with the flowerpot bread.

▶

for the flowerpot bread
makes 10 loaves

10 small terracotta flowerpots, 4" diameter

vegetable oil

750 g/1½ lb strong white flour

25 g/1 oz lard

1 tspn salt

sachet of dried yeast

1 tspn Italian dried mixed herb seasoning

450 ml/¾ pint warm water

1 egg, beaten, to glaze

sesame or poppy seeds, to decorate

to make the flowerpot bread

1 Preheat the oven to 180°C/350°F/Gas mark 4. Brush the inside of ten small, clean terracotta flowerpots with vegetable oil. Put in the hot oven to prove. Remove after 15 minutes and leave to cool. Once cool, brush again with oil and repeat the process four times. It is very important to let the pots cool before brushing with more oil.

2 Turn up the oven to 220°C/425°F/Gas mark 7. If using a mixer with a dough-hook attachment, put the flour and lard in the bowl with the salt, dried yeast and seasoning. Turn the mixer to minimum speed and add warm water slowly. Allow to knead on slow speed for about 4 minutes.

3 If making dough by hand, rub together the flour and lard in a bowl and add the salt, dried yeast and seasoning. Add the warm water slowly. Mix together to form a dough. Knead the dough on a floured work surface for about 10 minutes.

4 Separate the dough into ten pieces and put into the flowerpots. Leave in a warm place to prove, covered with cling film, to prevent a skin from forming.

5 Once the dough has doubled in size and risen to the top of the pots, brush with beaten egg and sprinkle with poppy or sesame seeds. Put the bread in the oven, turn down the heat to 200°C/400°F/Gas Mark 6 and bake for 20–25 minutes, till golden brown. (Preheating the oven temperature to higher than the desired baking temperature compensates for the heat lost when the oven door is opened to put the bread in for baking.) Check that the loaves are cooked by turning one out and checking it sounds hollow when tapped on the base.

Coronation Chicken

Pukka Polo Picnic – Emma Sturt

serves twelve

walnut oil, for frying

1.5 kg/3½ lb boneless, skinless chicken breasts, cubed or cut in bite-size strips

350 g/12 oz chutney

90 g/3 oz raisins

120 g/4 oz blanched almonds

2 tbspn curry paste

150 ml/¼ pint plain yoghurt

150 ml/¼ pint pot of soured cream

300 ml/½ pint mayonnaise

450 ml/¾ pint whipping cream

1 Heat the oil and fry the chicken quickly and thoroughly, being careful not to brown it. Allow to cool.

2 Mix all the other ingredients, except the whipping cream, in a large bowl.

3 Whip the cream until stiff. Fold the cream into the rest of the ingredients. Then coat the chicken pieces with the sauce.

Rosie's Placenta Pâté

Welcome to the World – Sue O'Neil

This dish must be the single most controversial item ever prepared on a cookery programme and is certainly the one I am most often asked about. The favourite question is, 'What did it taste like?' The answer is, 'surprisingly good,' it tastes rather like a coarse liver pâté, but with a milder taste. The second favourite question is, 'Were they mad?!' To which my reply is, 'not at all'. Rosie, mother of Indie-Mo and former 'owner' of the placenta, Rosie's mum, Mary and their best friend Sue, (who did the cooking) were lovely, warm people who knew exactly what they were doing and why they wanted to do it. (Now, as then, it's not for me to explain or justify their actions on their behalf.) Anyone who watched the programme rather than just listened to the gossip, could see that they were not sensation-seekers. I must admit I enjoyed the controversy it created partly because I find the whole subject of food taboos fascinating and partly because I enjoy the idea of pompous people getting hot under the collar with steam coming out of their ears, without actually being able to put their finger on what it is they are so upset about.

serves ten

1 placenta

2 tbspn olive oil

2 shallots, chopped

2 garlic cloves, chopped

2 tbspn brandy

50 g/2 oz butter, softened

1 tbspn each chopped fresh sage and parsley

juice of ½ lime

salt and pepper

crackers or buttered toast, to serve

1 Prepare the placenta by running it under cold water for a few minutes, to remove any blood. Remove the tough outer membrane. Chop into small chunks.

2 Heat the oil in a frying-pan. Add the shallots and garlic and then the placenta chunks. Fry until browned.

3 When nearly cooked, flambé with the brandy, tilting the pan to coat everything evenly. When the flames have died down, remove from the heat.

4 Purée half, with the softened butter and chopped herbs.

5 Chop the remaining portion very finely and add to the blended mixture. Add the lime juice, season to taste and serve on crackers or small pieces of buttered toast.

Terrine of Sweetbreads with Morels

Mushroom Magic – Bob Wootton

serves eight

750 g/1½ lb calves' sweetbreads

25 g/1 oz dried morels

1 egg, beaten

50 g/2 oz white breadcrumbs, soaked in a little milk

120 g/4 oz minced veal

salt and pepper

120 g/4 oz thinly sliced pancetta

50 g/2 oz butter

Madeira

20 juniper berries

10 black peppercorns

toasted brioche and green salad leaves, dressed with balsamic vinegar, to serve

1 Prepare the sweetbreads by soaking them in cold, salted water for at least 2 hours. Meanwhile, reconstitute the dried morels by soaking them in boiled water to cover for at least 20 minutes. Drain (the strained soaking water can be frozen as an excellent mushroom stock). Preheat the oven to 150°C/300°F/Gas mark 3.

2 Purée one of the smaller lobes of sweetbread with the egg, breadcrumbs, veal mince and salt and pepper to taste, to make a forcemeat. Blanch the remaining sweetbreads in fresh, salted water for 4 minutes and then break into pieces, pulling any remaining membranes away with your fingers.

3 Line a terrine dish (preferably a folding one) with cling film – don't worry, it won't burn! – and then line it again with overlapping strips of pancetta. Fry any leftover pancetta trimmings to give a crispy chef's perk and to extract the fat.

4 Slice and sauté the sweetbread lobes in the butter and resulting pancetta fat until slightly brown at the edges. Remove the sweetbreads and deglaze the pan with a splash of Madeira.

5 Pound the juniper berries and peppercorns in a pestle and mortar.

6 Assemble the terrine. First, put a thin layer of forcemeat in the bottom of the terrine. Then arrange pieces of sweetbread tightly in a layer on top. Sprinkle over a layer of the morels and season with pounded juniper berries and peppercorns. Repeat another two layers thus, pressing down frequently to ensure the terrine is

▶

well packed. Finish with a thin layer of the forcemeat, which acts as a 'cement'. Finally, pour over the deglazed pan juices and cover with the last of the pancetta slices.

7 Put the terrine dish in a roasting tin and pour in hot water to come to halfway up the sides of the terrine, to make a bain-marie. Bake for 90 minutes. Remove and leave to cool. Weight down and refrigerate for at least 12 hours.

8 One hour before serving, turn out the terrine using the cling film as a cradle (this is much easier if your dish is one of the dismantling kind). Put on a board and very carefully cut in 5 mm/¼ in slices. Serve the terrine with toasted brioche and green salad leaves, dressed with balsamic vinegar.

Scotch Eggs
A Nice Bit of Brisket – Josie Livingstone

serves four

4 large eggs

plain flour, sifted, for coating

900 g/2 lb fresh sausagemeat

60 g/2 oz each of breadcrumbs and porridge oats, for coating

oil, for deep-frying

small piece of bread

1 From cold, boil the eggs for 10–13 minutes. Run them under the cold tap so that no black edge appears round the yolks. Shell and dry them.

2 Roll the eggs in the flour.

3 Using wet hands, work a generous amount of sausagemeat round each egg, to coat it entirely.

4 Roll in the breadcrumb and oat mixture.

5 Heat the oil in a deep-fryer or a large, deep saucepan. Test the heat of the oil with a small piece of bread: it should cook to golden in about a minute. (You don't want the oil to be too hot or the meat won't cook evenly.)

6 Deep-fry two eggs at a time for 7–8 minutes. Drain on kitchen paper and serve cold, with a bit of salad.

Stuffed Quail with Gooseberry Marmalade

Colin and Duncan's Black Tie Dinner – Colin Beattie

serves eight

16 quails, boned

olive oil

salt and pepper

white wine

2–3 tbspn double cream

for the stuffing

3 tbspn olive oil

1½ peppers, seeded and finely chopped

3 cloves of garlic, crushed

1 medium onion, finely chopped

75 g/3 oz pine nuts

salt and pepper

for the gooseberry marmalade

500 g/1 lb gooseberries

1 medium onion, finely chopped

60 ml/4 tbspn cider

120 g/4 oz brown sugar

2 tspn balsamic vinegar

salt and pepper

1 Preheat the oven to 220°C/425°F/Gas mark 7. To make the stuffing, heat the oil in a pan and fry the peppers, garlic and onions gently until soft and golden.

2 Add the pine nuts and cook for a further 10 minutes. Season to taste.

3 Make the marmalade by putting all the ingredients in a heavy-based pan and simmering gently until the fruit is soft and the liquid has reduced. Season to taste and keep warm.

4 Take each bird and open out, scraping off meat from the excess skin areas. Place this meat in the centre of each bird.

5 Fill the cavity with stuffing and close the edges with a cocktail stick. Place, breast-side up, in a shallow roasting tin. Rub the skins lightly with a little oil and salt, to crisp them. Pour in enough white wine to cover the bottom of the dish and roast for 20–25 minutes.

6 Keep the birds warm on a serving dish. Reduce the pan juices, adding cream to thicken the sauce. Check the seasoning.

7 Serve two birds per person, with a little sauce and some warmed marmalade on the side.

Fried Chicken Livers in Ginger

Chinese Challenge – Gary Venables

serves six

375 g/12 oz fresh chicken livers

45 g/1½ oz plain flour

250 ml/8 fl oz groundnut oil

chopped fresh coriander, to garnish

for the marinade

¼ tspn salt

3 tspn finely chopped garlic

1½ tspn finely chopped fresh root ginger

1½ tbspn finely chopped spring onions

½ tspn sugar

1 tspn sesame oil

for the sauce

2 tspn finely chopped fresh root ginger

2 tspn light soy sauce

1½ tspn rice wine

1½ tspn Chinese white-rice wine vinegar

½ tspn sugar

1½ tspn sesame oil

1 Clean the livers and discard any membranes. Dry them well on kitchen paper and combine with the marinade ingredients; let the mixture marinate for 30–40 minutes.

2 Remove the livers from the marinade with a slotted spoon, dry them with kitchen paper and lightly dust with the plain flour.

3 Heat the oil in a wok until it is hot and then stir-fry the livers, in small batches, until they are crisp and brown. Drain the livers on kitchen paper.

4 Reserve about 1 tbspn of the oil in which you have cooked the livers, discard the rest and clean the wok. Fry the ginger in the reserved oil for a few seconds. Add the other sauce ingredients and bring to a simmer.

5 Return the livers to the wok and continue to stir-fry them for about 4 minutes; they should be thoroughly coated in the sauce and firm to the touch.

6 Serve immediately, with lots of fresh coriander to garnish.

Guinea-fowl Sausages with Normandy Sauce

A Literary Dinner – Lorna Macleod

Lorna is a self-confessed and somewhat self-deprecating, 'Hyacinth Bucket'-style hostess. In fact her guests adore her and devour her consistently posh nosh with great enthusiasm. Lorna has her sights set on Michelin stars – this recipe is from Raymond Blanc, no less.

makes twenty-four sausages, to serve twelve

for the mousse

1 poultry liver, washed and dried (guinea-fowl, chicken or duck)

milk

2 shallots, finely chopped

1 tspn unsalted butter, plus extra for frying

25 g/1 oz fresh breadcrumbs, soaked in a little milk

130 g/4½ oz back fat

200 g/7 oz guinea-fowl breast meat, diced

salt and pepper

1 egg

1 tspn Calvados

pinch of grated nutmeg

few leaves of fresh tarragon, finely chopped

1 clove, crushed

120 ml/4 fl oz whipping cream

4 m/13 ft natural sausage casing

to make the mousse

1 Soak the poultry liver in milk for 30 minutes; drain and pat dry. Sweat the shallot in the butter and 3 tbspn water for about 10 minutes, or until the water has completely evaporated. Squeeze out some of the milk from the breadcrumbs.

2 Grind the back fat into a paste and then add the diced guinea-fowl breast; season with a little salt and pepper and mix. Add the egg, Calvados, liver, breadcrumbs, shallots, nutmeg, tarragon and clove and mix thoroughly until smooth.

3 When completely mixed, pass the mixture through a fine sieve. Chill the mixture for 30 minutes. Slowly add the cream. Mix gently to start with and then beat vigorously, incorporating as much air as possible. Chill for at least an hour.

to make the sausages

1 Put the sausage casing over the cold tap and allow water to run through it for a few minutes; then cut into 30 cm/12 in lengths. Fit a large, plain nozzle into a pastry bag. Hold the sausage casing securely over the nozzle and fill with the chilled mousse. When it is full, tie a knot at both ends. (Do not tie a knot at one end before filling the casing as this will cause air bubbles.) Repeat with the remaining lengths of casing. Chill the sausages.

▶

2 Simmer the sausages in plenty of water for 20 minutes; drain then allow to cool completely. Cut open the ends with scissors and run a sharp knife down one side. Peel back the casing very carefully. Chill.

for the breadcrumb coating

50 g/2 oz whole hazelnuts, shelled
50 g/2 oz ground almonds
75 g/3 oz dried white breadcrumbs
salt and pepper
2 tbspn clarified butter

for the Normandy sauce

1 shallot, finely chopped
30 g/1oz unsalted butter
2 tbspn Calvados
200 ml/7 fl oz dry white wine
Dijon mustard
450 ml/¾ pint crème fraîche
shredded fresh tarragon leaves
salt and pepper

to garnish

60 g/2 oz unsalted butter, plus a little oil to prevent burning for frying
dessert apple quarters

to make the breadcrumb coating

1 Toast the hazelnuts for 5 minutes, until golden. Crush to a paste. Mix with the ground almonds and breadcrumbs in a shallow dish. Season.
2 Melt the clarified butter and carefully roll each sausage in it. Then roll gently in the breadcrumb and nut mixture. Chill for at least 30 minutes.

to cook the sausages and apples

1 Preheat the oven to 170°C/325°F/Gas mark 3. Heat the butter and fry the sausages, turning them until golden brown. Keep warm in the oven.
2 Melt the butter and fry the apples until caramelized (do not allow them to go soft; a blow torch can be used to brown the outsides, if the apples are starting to soften); set aside.

to make the sauce

1 Cook the shallot in the butter until golden; then pour off the remaining fat and deglaze the pan with Calvados, then wine. Reduce thoroughly and stir in the mustard and crème fraîche. Reduce the sauce again until it has a rich consistency. Add the shredded tarragon leaves and season to taste.

to serve

1 Place the sausages in the centre of a serving dish and pour the sauce over. Decorate with the apple pieces and serve.

Summer Rolls

First House-warming Vietnam-Style – Thi Nguyen

**serves twelve
(makes 24 rolls)**

for wrapping the rolls

500 g/1 lb packet of medium-
size rice paper sheets

for the pickled cabbage

½ cabbage

1 tbspn salt

1 carrot, peeled and grated

3 dspn cold water

2 tspn phu quoc or
Thai fish sauce

3 tspn sugar

2 cloves of garlic, finely
chopped

2 fresh red chillies, seeded and
finely chopped

3–4 dspn rice vinegar

for the pork and chicken

450 g/1 lb boneless
leg of pork

500 g/1 lb boneless chicken
breasts and thighs

1 vegetable stock cube

2 tspn sea salt

10 slices of fresh root ginger

1 tspn phu quoc or
Thai fish sauce

to make the pickled cabbage

1 Prepare the cabbage the night before: cut it into long, thin slices, cover with cold water and add 1 tspn salt. Allow to soak for 3 hours.
2 Wash away the salted water with plenty of cold water.
3 Squeeze the cabbage of its juice in between your hands, to dry it. Add the grated carrot, mix well and leave in a well sealed container at room temperature.
4 Put the water into a bowl and add the sugar, vinegar, chillies, garlic and fish sauce. Mix well and add to the cabbage and carrot mixture.

to cook the chicken and pork

1 Wash the pork and chicken in cold water, adding 2 teaspoons of salt.
2 Put the chicken and the pork into a large, flameproof casserole dish and pour water over to cover just half of the meat.
3 Add the vegetable stock cube, salt, slices of ginger, and fish sauce to the casserole.
4 Heat the water to boiling point and then turn down the heat and simmer for 30 minutes.
5 Test the meat and, if it is not cooked, turn it upside-down and cook for a further 30 minutes.
6 Remove the chicken and pork from the stock and leave to cool. (The stock can be used for soup.)
7 Discard the skin from the meat and slice the chicken and pork lengthways.

▶

for the 'pancakes'

5 eggs, beaten

groundnut oil, for frying

to make the 'pancakes'

1 Beat 5 eggs in a bowl.
2 Pour some egg into pan and fry like a pancake.
3 Repeat the process until the egg is used up.
4 Leave the 'pancakes' to cool and then slice them into long strips.

for the rice noodles

300 g/10 oz packet of rice noodles

to cook the rice noodles

1 Pour cold water over the rice noodles and allow to soak for 2 hours. Drain well.
2 Bring a large pan of water to the boil and add the noodles.
3 Immediately turn off the heat and leave the noodles in water for 1 minute.
4 Stir well and then leave in the water for another 3 minutes before draining.

for the vegetables

10 spring onions

small bunch of fresh mint and sweet basil

small bunch of fresh coriander

to prepare the spring onions and other fillings

1 Slice the spring onions lengthways into slender strips, using only the white part.
2 Pick off nice leaves of mint and basil for the rolls. Chop the coriander into 8 cm/3 in lengths.

for the peanuts

100 g/3½ oz shelled raw peanuts

to cook the peanuts

1 Add the peanuts to a dry wok and stir all the time, until they start to take colour.
2 Turn the heat down and keep stirring until they turn light brown.
3 Put the peanuts into a newspaper and wrap them up well – the peanuts will keep cooking.
4 Remove the papery skins from the peanuts and chop the nuts finely.

▶

to fill the rice paper

1 Prepare a big container of cold water. Rice paper is very dry and breaks easily. Put each rice paper in cold water, making sure that the whole surface of the paper is well soaked.

2 Wait until the paper goes soft, approximately 1 minute.

3 Put the spring onions, peanuts, noodles, coriander, mint, sweet basil, pork, chicken, egg pancake and cabbage into individual bowls.

4 Put a small amount of sliced pork and chicken in the centre of a piece of rice paper, adding some of the above ingredients, and then roll up the rice paper. The knack is to put a very small amount into each one. Fold the left- and right-hand corners in and then roll the paper up very tightly.

5 Place on a plate. Repeat above steps to fill all the sheets of rice paper, or until filling mixture runs out.

6 Do not refrigerate, but serve at room temperature as soon as possible.

Devilled Kidneys

Empire Club Breakfast – Duncan Douglas

serves six

butter, for frying

8 lamb's kidneys, cored and cut into bite-size pieces

1 tbspn brandy

4 shallots, finely chopped

75 ml/3 fl oz white wine

300 ml/½ pint chicken stock, reduced to 4 tbspn by simmering

150 ml/¼ pint double cream

¼–½ tspn cayenne pepper

1 tspn Worcestershire sauce

Tabasco sauce

freshly ground black pepper

to garnish

lightly buttered toast, to serve

chopped seeded fresh red and green chillies

chopped fresh parsley

1 Melt a large knob of butter in a heavy-based frying-pan. Add the kidneys once a high heat is reached and cook for 4–5 minutes.

2 Add the brandy and set light to the mixture to flambé the kidneys. Tilt the pan carefully from side to side until the flames die down. Remove the kidneys from the pan and keep warm.

3 To the remaining sauce, with a slotted spoon add the shallots and cook for 3–4 minutes, until they are translucent. Add the wine. Stir well to deglaze the pan and cook for a few minutes, until somewhat thickened.

4 Add the chicken stock and cook for 1 minute. Add the cream, cayenne pepper, worcestershire sauce and 4–5 drops of Tabasco and season to taste with black pepper.

5 Add the kidneys and heat through. Serve on lightly buttered toast, with crusts cut off, topped with finely chopped red and green chillies and chopped parsley.

Vegetarian

Gilded Pears with Goat's Cheese

Gordon's Table – Gordon Perrier

This dish was a direct celebration of the arrival of the new table (which is made from pear wood). The gold leaf, a touch of opulence, is edible but does not taste of much! The pears can be gilded in advance, but the goat's cheese should be grilled just before serving, so it is creamy and melted just underneath the breadcrumbs, but still cool and crumbly in the middle.

serves eight

8 ripe dessert pears

1 egg white

8 small sheets of transfer gold leaf (23¾ carat)

4 handfuls of dried white breadcrumbs (slices of stale white bread baked until hard and then pulverized)

pinch of ground cumin

pinch of ground coriander

2 tbspn poppy seeds

8 small whole goat's cheeses

1 egg, beaten

8 thick slices of ciabatta, brushed with walnut oil

8 sprigs of fresh coriander

4 tbspn hazelnut oil

1 Brush the base of each pear with egg white and leave for a few minutes to become tacky. Press the wax paper on which the gold leaf is mounted, on to the base of each pear so that the gold leaf is pressed on to the egg white. Holding each pear over a pudding plate, peel off the waxed paper and the excess leaf will float around the plate. Put each pear on a separate plate.

2 Heat a grill to high.

3 Mix the breadcrumbs, cumin, coriander and poppy seeds together.

4 Dip each goat's cheese into the beaten egg, coating it all over. Roll in the spiced breadcrumbs. Arrange the eight cheeses on the grill pan.

5 Toast one side of the cheeses under the grill for a couple of minutes so that the breadcrumbs are lightly browned. Turn over the cheeses and repeat.

6 Arrange a toasted goat's cheese, a slice of ciabatta and a sprig of coriander on each plate, next to the pear. Drizzle ½ tbspn hazelnut oil around each plate.

Haricot Vert Pakoras

Five Nations Rugby Curry – Gerry Mansfield

serves fifteen

packet of 'Gits' pakora batter mix (available from most Indian grocers)

1 tspn fennel seeds

good pinch of ground cumin

1 tspn chilli powder

½ tspn salt

1.5 kg/3½ lb fresh haricot verts (dwarf beans)

ghee or oil, for deep-frying

1 Make up the pakora mix to make about 1 litre/1¾ pints of batter. Mix in the fennel seeds, cumin, chilli powder and salt. Leave to stand for a few minutes.

2 In the meantime, top and tail the haricot verts. Rinse and pat dry.

3 Heat the ghee or oil in a chip pan or wok to frying temperature. Dunk the beans into the batter mix and deep-fry them for about 2 minutes, until lightly browned. Fry a few at a time, to prevent them from sticking together. Drain on kitchen paper before arranging on a warmed serving dish. Serve at once.

Matt's Sprouted Bean Feast

Getting into the Raw – Matt Fraser

serves six

4 mangos

375 g/12 oz sprouted beans, e.g. mung, aduki or lentil

250 g/8 oz sprouted alfafa or radish seeds

6 portions of goat's cheese

for the mustard vinaigrette

2 tbspn white-wine vinegar

2 tspn Dijon mustard

salt and pepper

6 tbspn olive oil

1 Remove the stones from the mangos and cut the flesh into slices, trimming the skin off with a sharp knife. Cut each slice into strips and divide between six plates. Place a selection of the sprouted beans and seeds on each plate alongside the mango and add a portion of goat's cheese.

2 Make the vinaigrette by combining the vinegar, mustard and seasoning in a small bowl. Gradually whisk in the oil in a steady stream, until smooth. (If the emulsion starts to curdle it can be reformed by rapid whisking.) Drizzle the vinaigrette over the mango and beansprouts and serve immediately.

Vegetable Terrine

A Vegan Theatre Picnic – Rachel Markham

serves six to eight

175 g/6 oz frozen spinach

175 g/6 oz frozen peas

175 g/6 oz carrots

175 g/6 oz cauliflower

1 tbspn lemon juice

1 tspn fresh ginger juice

1 tbspn chopped fresh chives

1 tbspn grated nutmeg

75 g/3 oz ground almonds

1 tbspn chopped fresh coriander

about 4 tbspn light tahini, to bind

salt and pepper

extra herbs and cherry tomatoes, to garnish

1 Preheat the oven to 190°C/375°F/Gas mark 5.
2 Steam each vegetable separately.
3 Purée each vegetable, adding 1 tspn of lemon juice each to the pea, spinach and carrot purées and 1 tspn ginger juice to the cauliflower purée.
4 Stir the chopped chives into the pea mixture, the nutmeg into the spinach mixture, the ground almonds into the carrot mixture and the fresh coriander into the cauliflower mixture.
5 Add about 1 tbspn of tahini to each mixture and stir well to bind. Season to taste with salt and pepper.
6 Fully line a 450 g/1 lb loaf tin with baking parchment.
7 Spoon the pea purée into the tin and smooth down. Repeat with the carrot, cauliflower and spinach purées.
8 Cover the terrine with oiled baking parchment and place in a roasting tin. Pour in hot water to come about halfway up the sides of the terrine. Bake for about an hour, until firm to the touch.
9 Remove from the oven and leave to cool before turning out on to a serving plate. Garnish with herbs and cherry tomatoes.

Onion and Goat's Cheese Tarts with Walnut Pastry

Late Starter – Wendy Ingham

An inventive savoury version of tarte tatin.

serves six, as a starter

50 g/2 oz butter

1 kg/2¼ lb red onions, very thinly sliced

2 tbspn olive oil

100 ml/3½ fl oz white wine

1 tbspn white-wine vinegar

1 tspn chopped fresh thyme or ½ tspn dried

salt and freshly ground black pepper

300 g/10 oz puff pastry

3–4 tbspn finely chopped walnuts

3 tomatoes, thinly sliced

120 g/4 oz goat's cheese log, finely diced

6 tspn walnut oil, plus extra to serve

baby salad leaves and whole walnuts, to serve

1 Grease six small individual tart dishes with butter.

2 Melt the butter and fry the onions very gently in the butter and olive oil for about 10 minutes, stirring occasionally with a wooden spoon or spatula, until soft and golden (do not allow to burn).

3 Add the wine, white-wine vinegar and thyme and cook until all the liquid has evaporated. Season with salt and pepper.

4 Divide the pastry into three, sprinkling each piece with the walnuts, then stack the pieces on top of each other and roll out thinly.

5 Cut six discs of pastry to the size of the tart dishes, then place in the fridge for 30 minutes to rest.

6 Preheat the oven to 220°C/425°F/Gas mark 7.

7 Place a few slices of tomato on the bottom of each dish and then divide the onion mixture between the dishes.

8 Place a disc of pastry over the onion mixture and tuck the edges in. Prick all over with a fork to help to keep the pastry crisp.

9 Place in the middle of the preheated oven for 15 minutes, until risen and golden.

10 Remove from the oven and put a plate over each tart dish. Invert and shake firmly.

11 Slide each tart on to a greased baking sheet and sprinkle with goat's cheese and the walnut oil. Place under a preheated grill to melt the cheese.

12 To serve, accompany with a crisp salad of baby leaves, sprinkled with a few walnuts and a further drizzle of walnut oil.

Grilled Polenta with Wild Mushrooms and Red Onions

Tuscany-by-Doncaster – Michael Masserella

Polenta is a supremely versatile staple food in Italy, simple but much loved. Michael's friend Letitzia Bergomi serves it 'wet' – straight from the saucepan – with a fresh boiling sausage and plenty of butter and Parmesan. And every time she mounds up a plate, her husband Adolpho's eyes light up. Originally a humble dish, polenta now features on menus in top restaurants all over the world. Michael admits it took him some time to take to polenta, but now he is addicted to its versatility and eats it hot and cold, in snacks, starters and main courses, spread with all sorts of toppings, from eggs to pesto to this red onion, mushroom and mozzarella one. An instant variety, available at some supermarkets, cooks in just a few minutes and thus takes the heavy elbow work out of the job.

serves six or eight, as part of a buffet

500 g/1 lb bag of real or instant polenta

4 red onions, thinly sliced

1 tbspn oil

15 g/½ oz butter

500 g/1 lb mushrooms (wild or a mixture of wild and cultivated), peeled or washed and sliced

2 handfuls of fresh herbs, such as oregano, parsley and basil, finely chopped

120 g/4 oz mozzarella cheese

1 In a large pan, bring 2 litres/3½ pints of salted water up to the boil, then lower the heat so it is gently simmering. Pour in the polenta in a steady thin stream, stirring all the time with a wooden spoon. The polenta will start to thicken and bubble. To avoid the dreaded lumps, you must stir all the time in the same direction. If lumps should appear, don't panic – a little vigorous work with a balloon whisk should get rid of them. When the polenta starts to stiffen and pull away from the pan sides (after 25–35 minutes) it is ready. If you are using instant polenta, follow the pack instructions.

2 When cooked, pour the polenta into a shallow rectangular dish or tray and spread with a spatula to a depth of about 2–3 cm/1–1¼ in. Leave to go cold.

▶

3 Fry the sliced red onions in a pan with oil and butter until soft but not over-browned. Add the mushrooms and continue cooking until their juices have been released and sweated off. Set aside.

4 Cut the cold polenta into shapes (squares, circles, rectangles, etc.), larger or smaller, depending on whether you are serving them as canapés, starters or a main course.

5 Top each piece of polenta with the onion and mushroom mixture. Sprinkle with herbs. Place a little piece of mozzarella cheese on top and flash under the grill or place in a hot oven (220°C/425°F/Gas mark 7) until brown and bubbling.

6 Serve at once, but warn the greedy not to burn their mouths.

Main courses

Fish

Squid stuffed with Fetta Cheese and Mushrooms
Ancient Greek Symposium – Dimitris Vassilliou

serves six

12 fresh squid, bodies only, cleaned but left whole

olive oil

juice of 2 lemons

12 lemon wedges, to serve

for the stuffing

5 tbspn olive oil

sprig of fresh rosemary

2 large onions, chopped

8 cloves of garlic, chopped

250 g/8 oz mushrooms, chopped

juice of 1½ lemons

½ bottle of dry white wine

120 g/4 oz dried breadcrumbs

375 g/12 oz fetta cheese

freshly ground black pepper

12 tbspn chopped fresh parsley

1 tspn chopped fresh thyme

1 tspn chopped fresh tarragon

1. To make the stuffing, heat the oil in a frying-pan, fry the rosemary sprig for 30 seconds and then set it aside.

2. Fry the chopped onions and garlic until soft. Add the mushrooms and cook for 3 minutes. Add the lemon juice and wine, stir and reduce a little over a medium heat. Add the breadcrumbs, cheese and pepper. Stir in the parsley, thyme and tarragon and take off the heat.

3. Make sure the stuffing is well packed into the squid. Secure with a toothpick. Brush each squid with olive oil and a squeeze of lemon juice.

4. To cook, either heat up a griddle or skillet pan and sear the squid on each side, or grill under a pre-heated grill for 5 minutes. Do not overcook. Serve with a wedge of lemon.

Clare Montcrieff-Hunt's Crab, Coconut and Coriander Soup

Marguerite Vincent's Pissaladière Canapés

Jon Ashton's Black Pudding Wontons with Balsamic Sauce

Ozi Osmond's Cockles and Laverbread

Colin Beattie's Stuffed Quail with Gooseberry Marmalade

Dimitris Vassilliou's Squid stuffed with Fetta Cheese and Mushrooms

Selina Snow's Sea Bass baked with Fennel, Lemon and Thyme with Saffron and Lemon Mayonnaise

Duncan Douglas' Breakfast Kebab

Bandaged Fish

A Futurist Feast – Celia Lyttleton

*A curious dish which, after the unpredictable manner of Futurist
feasts, Celia served not as a course but as a tantalizer. After the
elaborate preparation (the fish is stuffed as well as wrapped), the
dish was passed around the guests for admiration, then whisked
away, never to be seen again. Except, that is, by me. I ate one in
the kitchen and found it delicious, though I wouldn't necessarily
recommend you serve it on a bed of green jelly!*

serves six

1 packet of green jelly

6 strips of nori seaweed

mirin wine

3 handfuls of pine nuts

sprig of fresh rosemary

about 12 seedless white grapes

salt and freshly ground
black pepper

6 red mullets, approximately
250 g/8 oz each, gutted
and scaled

1 Make up the green jelly according to the packet
   instructions and put in the fridge to set.

2 Put the strips of seaweed in a pan and add a
   slosh of the mirin wine and enough water to
   cover. Bring to the boil, then simmer for a few
   minutes, until soft and pliable.

3 Toast the pine nuts in a dry frying-pan with the
   rosemary, taking care not to burn them.

4 Discard the rosemary sprig and then whizz the
   nuts in a food processor to a coarse paste.

5 Slice the grapes into slivers. Mix gently with the
   pine-nut mixture. Season with salt and pepper.

6 Stuff the gutted fish with the pine-nut and
   grape mixture.

7 Put the fish on a ridged griddle pan or under a
   hot grill and cook on both sides, until done.

8 Wrap a piece of cooked seaweed around
   each fish.

9 Roughly chop the jelly and spread on a platter
   or large serving plate to make a 'sea'.

10 Arrange the fish on the jelly.

11 If at a Futurist feast, present these beautiful fish to
    your hungry guests, then whisk them away again
    immediately! Otherwise forget the jelly, and
    serve and eat them as they are.

Squid with Noodles and Vegetable Tentacles

Rumble in the Jungle – Felicity Keebaugh

'Always go to the main source' is Felicity's philosophy in life and the same holds true in cooking, so she makes use of the diversity of ethnic shops in London. The fresh egg noodles and soy sauces used to make this recipe come from a local Chinese store, where the produce is fresh and cheap – and cooking tips come for free.

A Note on Buying Squid

Squid come in many sizes. Choose one, two or three per person according to size and your guests' appetites. Look for the small squid from the Mediterranean, sometimes called calamares which are about 8–12 cm/3–5 in long and very tender. If you can't get them, just buy the smallest fresh squid you can find. The fishmonger should clean them for you – ask for the body to be left whole but they are really quite easy to clean yourself (see the instructions on page 75). If the squid are on the large side, they may be tough. Felicity's Antipodean tip for tenderizing them is to put them in a plastic bag in the fridge with a mashed-up kiwi fruit for an hour.

serves six

250 g/8 oz fresh or dried egg noodles

3 tbspn thick sweet soy sauce

2 tbspn ordinary dark soy sauce

3 long, thin leeks

2 long red peppers

75 g/3 oz butter

salt and freshly ground black pepper

1 clove of garlic, finely chopped

6–18 small squid (depending on size), body only, cleaned but kept whole

1 If using dried noodles, blanch in boiling water for just a minute to tenderize. Soak the noodles in the thick and dark soy sauces for 20 minutes. They will start to turn a deep brown.

2 Transfer the noodles and sauce to a pan and heat gently for 5–10 minutes, turning once or twice (tongs are the best tool) and adding just a little water if they seem to be sticking together, until the noodles are a rich mahogany colour, and tender.

3 Cut the leeks and the peppers into strips, as long and thin as possible. Cook in a steamer (or in a large saucepan with just a little water) until tender and then add 25 g/1 oz butter, salt and pepper.

▶

1 kiwi fruit
(optional – see note above)

1 large, wide cucumber, peeled
and very finely sliced diagonally

Thai sweet red chilli dipping
sauce, to serve

4 Melt 50 g/2 oz butter and add the garlic. Fry the squid for a few minutes. Timing depends on size and they will shrink as they cook.

5 Take six dinner plates, white if possible, and cover each with slightly overlapping layers of pale green cucumber. Divide the squid between the plates, then twist the peppers, leeks and noodles together and put them all around, so they flow out as if in a swirl of multicoloured tentacles. Put a small cup of Thai sweet chilli dipping sauce in the centre of each plate.

Whole John Dory in Red Wine Sauce
Trawlerman's Supper – George Dyer

serves eight

8 medium-size John Dory

3–4 tbspn olive oil

2 small onions, roughly chopped

bunch of spring onions,
chopped

1 red pepper,
seeded and chopped

1 yellow pepper,
seeded and chopped

8 cloves of garlic, chopped

8–10 vine tomatoes,
roughly chopped

1 litre/1¾ pint tomato juice

½ bottle of red wine

4 heaped tbspn chopped
fresh parsley

4 heaped tbspn chopped
fresh coriander

5 red mullet heads

1 Preheat the oven to 180°C/375°F/Gas mark 4.

2 Trim the three spiky fins on the fish back to the body, with a pair of scissors. Remove the scales.

3 Heat the oil in a frying-pan and fry the onions and spring onions until soft. Add the peppers and garlic, tomatoes and tomato juice, red wine, parsley and coriander.

4 Add the fish heads and simmer for 10 minutes, until the fish skulls begin to emerge and the fish flakes off.

5 Push the juice through a fine sieve.

6 Pour the sauce into a pan large enough to hold the eight fish. Put in all eight fish – they can overlap each other but make sure the sauce submerges the fish. Bake for 40 minutes.

Grilled Shark Steaks, Marinated in Lime with Mole Sauce

The Chilli Boys – Eddie Baines and Steve Donovan

Shark is a strong, meaty fish which stands up well to the flavour of the mole sauce. Mexican mole sauces are all about the art of blending. A large number of powerfully flavoured ingredients are combined in such a way that all contribute but none predominates. In Mexico, mole is served on all special occasions. Steve and Eddie have adapted the classic mole for non-meat eaters, substituting chicken stock with Steve's home-made chilli beer (stout will do) and serving it with shark marinated in lime. This sauce can be made well in advance. It will keep for up to two weeks in the fridge and if anything improves over time.

serves four

2 x 400–500 g/14–16 oz shark steaks
-----
2 limes
-----
salt and freshly ground black pepper

1 Remove the skin and central cartilage from the shark steaks and cut each in half, to get four portions.

2 Grate the zest from the two limes sparingly – try to avoid scraping into the white pith, which is bitter. Squeeze the limes. Reserve a pinch of the zest and 1 tspn of the juice.

3 Marinate the fish in the rest of the lime juice and zest for not more than one hour (otherwise the fish will become too soft).

4 Heat a cast-iron grill pan (the kind with raised ridges is ideal) or heavy frying-pan until it is very hot. Wipe the excess marinade off the steaks and place them on the pan (unless you have a very large pan, you will probably be able to cook only two at a time). Cook for about 3 minutes on each side. Season with salt and pepper before and after turning.

5 Just before serving, dress each shark steak with a little extra lime juice and a pinch of zest.

▶

Note: The following procedure is the standard preparation for most dried chillies prior to cooking.

for the mole sauce

2 dried passilla chillies

2 dried mulato chillies

2 ancho chillies

5 tbspn sesame seeds

¼ tspn whole coriander seeds

1 star anise

2.5 cm/1 in cinnamon stick

3 whole cloves

1 tspn sunflower oil

50 g/2 oz whole almonds with skins

75 g/3 oz raisins

salt

1 tbspn tomato paste

1 small onion, finely chopped

45 g/1½ oz Mexican chocolate (or highest-grade dark chocolate)

300 ml/½ pint chilli ale 'Smoky Dog' (or good dark stout)

to make the mole sauce

1 On a dry cast-iron skillet (or heavy frying-pan), toast the chillies over a high heat for a few minutes, turning occasionally. Split open the chillies, remove the seeds and stalk and, using your fingernails or a small knife, pare off the thicker veins. Rinse well. Put the chillies into a bowl and pour over just enough boiling water to cover. Leave to soak for 30 minutes to an hour. Drain, reserving the soaking liquid.

2 Dry roast the sesame seeds over a medium heat in a skillet or heavy frying-pan until they begin to pop, stirring quickly. Remove from the pan. Put aside 2 tbspn of the seeds for decorating the end dish.

3 Dry roast the coriander seeds, star anise, cinnamon stick and cloves for a short while until they start to change colour and become fragrant (around 30 seconds). Remove from the pan.

4 Put a little sunflower oil into the skillet and toast the almonds for a few minutes, taking care not to burn them. Dry on some paper. Add the raisins to the pan and cook until they puff up. Dry on kitchen paper.

5 Grind together all the spices in a coffee grinder or pound with a pestle and mortar.

6 Put the ground spices in a blender and add the chillies, about half of the liquid in which they have been soaking, a large pinch of salt, the almonds, raisins, tomato paste and chopped onion. Whizz up in the blender to get a smooth paste.

7 Put the paste in a hot skillet and fry gently. Add the chocolate and the chilli beer or stout.

▶

8 Simmer the sauce slowly for about 45 minutes, stirring occasionally to prevent it sticking to the pan. If the sauce becomes too thick, add a little more beer or more of the chilli soaking water. You want to get a thick pouring consistency which slides off the spoon.

to serve

1 Put some sauce on each plate and scatter on the reserved sesame seeds and serve with shark marinated in lime. It is equally delicious with other simply grilled fish – particularly fresh swordfish or tuna – or with chicken or turkey.

'Salmon in the Sink'

Pukka Polo Picnic – Emma Sturt

serves ten

1.5 kg/3 lb whole salmon, scaled and cleaned

1 Clean and thoroughly rinse the sink and put in the plug.

2 Arrange the salmon as if swimming in an S shape in the sink.

3 Pour boiling water on to the salmon until it is covered by 8 cm/3 in. Place a double thickness of foil over the top, to seal the steam in.

4 For a 1.5 kg/3 lb salmon, leave in the sink to 'cook' for 1 hour.

5 Remove the salmon and straighten it out while hot. Slit the skin lengthways along the dorsal fin and peel the skin back and off gently. Turn the salmon over gently and repeat. Serve with fresh lime mayonnaise (see page 30), dill and mustard mayonnaise (page 38) or saffron and lemon mayonnaise (page 72).

Gumbo

Gumbo Loft Party – Brenlen Jinkens

serves eight

175 ml/6 fl oz vegetable oil

75 g/3 oz plain flour

4 onions, finely minced

8 spring onions, finely minced

5 stalks of celery, finely minced

4 green peppers, seeded and finely minced

2 bay leaves

2 tspn salt

½ tspn ground black pepper

½ tspn ground white pepper

½ tspn cayenne pepper

½ tspn dried thyme

½ tspn dried oregano

1dspn minced garlic

1.2 litres/2 pints seafood stock

500 g/1 lb smoked sausages, cut in 1 cm/½ in slices

500g/1 lb smoked ham, cut in thick chunks

500g/1 lb peeled raw tiger prawns

375 g/12 oz crabmeat

12 medium oysters

1 Heat the oil in a heavy pan over a high heat, until smoking. Gradually sprinkle in the flour, whisking constantly. Once all the flour is added, continue whisking constantly and cook until the roux is dark brown. This will take 2–4 minutes – allow it to go a very dark brown but do not let it burn.

2 As soon as the colour has turned, add the minced onions, spring onions, celery and green peppers and stir in thoroughly. Cook for 3–4 minutes and then add all the seasonings – the bay leaves, salt, black, white and cayenne peppers, thyme and oregano. Cook for a couple of minutes and then add the minced garlic. Cook for a minute and then remove from the heat.

3 In a separate large saucepan, bring the seafood stock to the boil and slowly add the roux mixture, a little at a time. Allow it to dissolve completely each time.

4 In a frying-pan, fry the smoked sausage and ham and then add them to the stock and roux mixture. Bring back to the boil and simmer for about 10 minutes. Add the prawns, crabmeat and oysters and bring back to the boil. Cook for about 10 minutes.

5 Serve the gumbo with rice. You can freeze it or keep it in the fridge – indeed, the flavour improves if you leave it until the next day before eating it.

Sea Bass baked with Fennel, Lemon and Thyme with Saffron and Lemon Mayonnaise

The French Connection – Selina Snow

This is the dish that put to the test Selina's theory that a day trip to Boulogne would land you a fresher fish than any London fishmonger. Having tasted the evidence, I can't dispute her claim. This recipe, improvised entirely by Selina (and certainly open to further improvisation by you), is one of many in this book that I have since cooked several times at home. I like to eat it cold, with the same saffron and lemon mayonnaise, as an outdoorsy summer dish. Cold sea bass is as good, if not better than cold salmon.

serves two

4 tbspn olive oil

2 small sea bass, approximately 350–400 g/ 12–14 oz each, gutted and scaled

2 bulbs of fennel, cut downwards into medium slices

bunch of fresh thyme

zest of 1 lemon

2 bay leaves

salt and freshly ground black pepper

1 Preheat the oven to 200°C/400°F/Gas mark 6.

2 Lightly rub a shallow baking dish with a little of the olive oil.

3 Stuff the fish with sliced fennel, a couple of sprigs of thyme, half the lemon zest and one bay leaf each. Scatter more thyme and the rest of the lemon zest above and below the fish. Season the fish well, inside and out, with salt and pepper, and trickle over the olive oil.

4 Loosely cover the dish with foil and place in the oven. After 10 minutes, remove the foil to crisp the skin. The fish should be ready 10 minutes later.

to make the mayonnaise

1 Put the egg yolk, soaked saffron threads, lemon zest, salt and pepper in a food processor and mix them well.

2 Keeping the motor going, drizzle in the oil very slowly. The mayonnaise will become thick and creamy.

3 Add lemon juice to taste and check the seasoning.

▶

for the mayonnaise

1–3 tspn lemon juice

yolk of 1 large
free-range egg

large pinch of saffron threads,
crushed and soaked in 2 tbspn
warm water

grated zest of 1 lemon

salt and pepper

150 ml/¼ pint extra-virgin olive
oil (or half and half olive and
sunflower oil)

4 If not using a food processor, put the egg yolk, saffron, lemon zest, salt and pepper into a mixing bowl and use a hand or electric whisk to mix them together. Whisk in the oil, a drop at a time, until about half the oil has been added and then in a slow, thin trickle for the rest of the oil.

to serve

1 Serve the sea bass with the mayonnaise and a warm potato and olive salad. The mayonnaise also goes well with any other hot or cold fish.

Seared Tuna

Ancient Greek Symposium – Dimitris Vassilliou

serves six

1 kg/2¼ lb tuna fillet

sesame oil

sesame seeds

large bunch of coriander,
chopped

Thai fish sauce

1 Smear the tuna with a little sesame oil. Roll the fillet in enough sesame seeds to give it a thin coating.

2 Heat up a skillet and, when hot enough, sear the tuna on both sides for a few minutes. Remove from the skillet and immediately put into the freezer compartment of the fridge. Leave to go very cold, but not frozen. Remove and slice three-quarters of the way through the flesh. Pack chopped coriander between the slices and on top of the tuna. Drizzle with Thai fish sauce and serve immediately.

Crab Callaloo

Hampstead Callaloo – Bobby Gangar

***serves twenty,
as part of a large spread***

200 g/7 oz block of coconut
cream

300 ml/½ pint water

2 medium-size fresh crabs

juice of 2 limes or lemons
(optional)

1 medium onion,
roughly chopped

2 cloves of garlic, crushed

1 tspn all-purpose seasoning or
meat seasoning

2 tbspn green seasoning
(see page 84)

500 g/1 lb fresh spinach,
washed and trimmed

250 g/8 oz okra,
cut in 1 cm/½ in lengths

1 small pumpkin or squash,
peeled, seeded and cut
in chunks

1 'scotch bonnet' pepper

salt and pepper

1 Place the block of coconut cream in a saucepan with the water and dissolve slowly over a gentle heat.

2 Trim the legs and claws from the crabs, remove the back (and discard), and chop the body in half. Wash everything in lime or lemon juice (this is a traditional Caribbean technique for cleaning meat or fish, but it is optional). Then rinse in water. Place in the bottom of a large pan.

3 Add the following ingredients, one at a time, in layers, in the order listed, seasoning with all-purpose and green seasoning between each layer: onions; garlic; spinach; okra; pumpkin or squash.

4 Pour in the prepared coconut cream and place the 'scotch bonnet' pepper (whole) on the top. Bring to the boil, without stirring, and then cover and simmer for half an hour.

5 Remove from the heat and discard the 'scotch bonnet' pepper. Using a 'swizzle stick' or hand-held blender, liquidize the callaloo, taking care to avoid the crab pieces in the bottom (it should resemble a thick, smooth soup).

6 Season to taste and serve with the crab pieces in the bottom of the dish, (each person should have a little of the crab).

Squid stuffed with Minced Pork, Shrimps and Mushrooms

Chinese Moon Festival – Rose Billaud

*The second of two stuffed squid dishes, this is the 'oriental' version.
I love them both, but then I'm a sucker for squid in just about
any form.*

serves fifteen to twenty

20 squid

3 tablespoons oil

2 cloves of garlic

salt

2 tbspn oyster sauce

1 tbspn light soy sauce

1 tspn sugar

400 g/14 oz tin of tomatoes

1 tspn cornflour,
mixed with a little water

for the stuffing

500 g/1 lb minced pork

10 medium-size shrimps,
cut in small pieces

5 dried Chinese mushrooms,
soaked in water and
finely chopped

5 spring onions, finely chopped

½ tspn salt

½ tspn pepper

½ tspn sesame oil

2 tbspn light soy sauce

1 Clean the squid by pulling off their heads, removing the skin and emptying their insides, leaving them like little pouches. Also retain the heads and tentacles. Or get your fishmonger to do this.

2 Mix all the stuffing ingredients together well in a bowl.

3 Stuff the squid with the filling, sealing them with toothpicks, piercing the ends twice.

4 Heat the oil in a wok and stir-fry the garlic with a little salt, just until the garlic starts to take colour.

5 Add the stuffed squid tentacles and heads, and stir-fry until brown. Add the oyster sauce, soy sauce and sugar.

6 Add the tomatoes and bring to the boil. Season with salt. Simmer for about 10 minutes.

7 Thicken the sauce with the cornflour mixture. Stir well until the sauce is smooth and thick. Serve hot, as soon as possible.

Stuffed Crabs

Gumbo Loft Party – Brenlen Jinkens

serves six

6 medium-size live crabs

2 litres/3¼ pints seafood stock

120 g/4 oz unsalted butter

4 dspn margarine

1 onion, finely minced

6 spring onions, finely minced

4 stalks of celery, minced

2 green peppers, seeded and finely minced

2 tspn minced garlic

1 tspn salt

1 tspn ground white pepper

1 tspn ground black pepper

1 tspn cayenne pepper

½ tspn dried thyme

approximately 120 g/4 oz fine dried breadcrumbs

1 Preheat the oven to 230°C/450°F/Gas mark 8. Fill the sink with cold water, add a generous amount of salt and place the crabs in the water for about 10 minutes.

2 Heat the seafood stock in a large pan over a high heat. Bring to the boil. Drain the crabs and add to the stock. Cover the pan and bring back to the boil. Reduce the heat and simmer for about 15 minutes. Check to see if any fat is coming to the surface – if there is, skim off and reserve it.

3 Remove the crabs from the pan and allow to cool. When they are cool enough to handle, remove the back shells and set aside. Remove the crabmeat and coral from the bodies and claws and set aside. Separate the brown meat and coral from the white meat. Remove the back of each shell and discard. Scrape out any residue and wash the shells thoroughly. Drain.

4 In a heavy-based, shallow pan, melt half the butter and the margarine over a high heat. Stir in the onion, spring onions, celery and green peppers and cook for a couple of minutes. Add the garlic and cook for a further 2 minutes. Add all the white meat and 1 tbspn of brown meat and the coral from the crabs and cook for about 4 minutes.

5 Combine the seasonings – salt, white, black and cayenne pepper, and thyme – and add to the pan. Cook for another 3–4 minutes, stirring frequently.

6 Add 175 ml/12 fl oz reduced seafood stock and cook for about 5 minutes, stirring constantly.

7 Add the breadcrumbs and stir in – the mixture should thicken up so that it forms a loose stuffing.

▶

If it is too liquid, add some more breadcrumbs until it comes together. Remove from the heat and stir in the remaining butter until it melts.

8 Stuff the cleaned crab shells with about half a cup of stuffing each. Place on an ungreased baking tray and bake for about 20–25 minutes, until a brown crust is formed. Serve immediately.

Whelks stuffed with Minced Pork

First House-warming Vietnam-style – Thi Nguyen

In Vietnam this dish is made from freshwater snails, but it works very well, we discovered, with good old English whelks. The whelks can be bought alive from a reliable fishmonger, or pre-cooked (in which case, follow the recipe from step 4).

serves twelve

24 whelks or freshwater snails

½ vegetable stock cube

120 g/4 oz minced pork

1 small bunch of spring onions (green part only), chopped

2 tspn fish sauce

5 pieces of dried black Chinese mushrooms, finely chopped

small bunch of fresh dill

5 stalks of lemongrass, cut in 8 cm/3 in pieces

1 Clean the whelks thoroughly with a scrubbing brush under a running cold tap.
2 An hour before eating, boil the whelks for approximately 10–20 minutes.
3 Pull the whelks or snails out of their shells.
4 Chop the whelk or snail flesh finely (do not put in a blender).
5 Dissolve the vegetable stock cube in a little boiling water to make a paste.
6 Combine the minced pork, whelks or snails, spring onions, fish sauce, dried mushrooms, vegetable stock paste and dill in a bowl.
7 Put the mixture on a chopping board and chop it really well together, until the mixture is quite smooth.
8 Take the lemongrass stalks and put one inside a shell, using a finger to press it well down to the bottom of the shell. Put some of the stuffing mixture in. Repeat with the remaining shells.
9 Steam the stuffed whelks or snails for 20–30 minutes. Serve with rice noodles.

Fresh Mackerel
in Plum Chutney Sauce

Cornish Fish Barbecue – Clare Montcrieff-Hunt

serves six

salt and pepper

juice of 2 lemons

6 medium or 12 small freshly-caught mackerel, gutted but heads left on

120 g/4 oz butter

750 g/1½ lb plum chutney, preferably home-made (recipe follows)

250 ml/8 fl oz white wine

for the sauce

makes enough to fill two 500 g/1 lb jars

1.5 kg/3 lb fresh ripe red plums, stoned

2 medium onions, chopped

2 medium apples, peeled, cored and chopped

2 tspn ground ginger

4 tspn ground cinnamon

4 tspn ground allspice

2 tbspn salt

600 ml/1 pint good wine vinegar

500 g/1 lb sugar

1 Sprinkle salt, pepper and lemon juice on each fish. Place under the grill or on the barbecue for a minute on each side.

2 Melt the butter in a large, heavy-based pan. Transfer the fish to the butter and add the plum chutney and wine. Simmer gently for 5–8 minutes (depending on the size of the fish).

to make the sauce

1 Put the plums, onions and apples in a large saucepan, with the spices, salt and half the wine vinegar. Bring to the boil and simmer for 45 minutes.

2 Gradually add the remainder of the vinegar until the mixture is thick and smooth.

3 Add the sugar and boil at a high temperature until the consistency is of jam. Pour into sterilized, warmed jars and seal.

to serve

1 Serve the fish with a large spoonful of the chutney sauce.

Meat

English Beef Vindaloo

Five Nations Rugby Curry – Gerry Mansfield

serves fifteen

4 kg/8 lb topside of English beef, fat removed and cubed

for the marinade

6 tbspn ground coriander

3 tbspn ground cumin

20 dried red chillies, broken into small pieces

3 tbspn black mustard seeds

2 tspn dried fenugreek seeds

4 tspn ground turmeric

12 cloves of garlic, crushed

2 tbspn chopped fresh root ginger

6 tbspn red-wine vinegar

generous 6 tbspn vodka

6 large onions, finely chopped

6 tbspn ghee

2 tbspn chilli powder

salt

900 ml/1½ pints water

20 small new potatoes, scrubbed and halved

chopped fresh coriander, to garnish

1 Combine all the spices (except the chilli powder and salt) with the garlic and ginger in a bowl. Add the wine vinegar and vodka to make a paste (adding more liquid if necessary). Add the cubed beef and mix well to fully coat all the pieces. Cover and leave to marinate in the refrigerator, preferably overnight.

2 In a large pan, fry the meat for 5 minutes, stirring occasionally. Cover and leave to cook in its own juices for 15 minutes, or until the liquid has reduced to a thick paste. Remove from the heat and set aside.

3 In a separate pan, fry the onions in the ghee until soft (about 5 minutes) and then add to the pan with the meat (pour in any ghee remaining in the pan). Add the chilli powder and salt and continue to stir-fry for another few minutes.

4 Add the water, bring to the boil, cover and simmer for 45–55 minutes or until the meat is almost tender. (Check the water level occasionally and top up, if necessary.)

5 Add the potatoes, stir and bring to the boil again. Cover and simmer for 15–20 minutes, until the potatoes are cooked. Serve garnished with chopped coriander, with rice.

Braised Oxtail with Celeriac

Wynne's Last Supper – Wynne Fearfield

For Wynne, cooking isn't just a hobby or an interest, it's an all-consuming obsession. She has around 300 cookbooks. This recipe is based on one from her trusty manual, **Leith's Cookery Bible,** by Prue Leith and Caroline Waldegrave.

serves six

2.7 kg/6 lb oxtail cut into pieces (the butcher will do this)

plain flour, seasoned

25 g/1 oz beef dripping or 2 tbspn oil

375 g/12 oz carrots, peeled and thickly sliced

250 g/8 oz onion, sliced

150 ml/¼ pint red wine

600 ml/1 pint veal or beef stock

4 sprigs of fresh thyme

1 bay leaf

½ tspn caster sugar

½ tspn tomato purée

juice of ½ lemon

salt and freshly ground black pepper

To accompany and garnish

900 g/2 lb celeriac, peeled and cut into 2 cm/1 in dice

1–2 tbspn oil

2 tbspn chopped fresh parsley

2 tbspn chopped fresh chives

1 Preheat the oven to 150°C/300°F/Gas mark 2.

2 Toss the oxtail pieces in the seasoned flour. Fry in the dripping or oil until well browned on all sides. Drain in a colander.

3 Brown the carrots and onion. Take care not to burn the vegetables or you may introduce a bitter note to the taste of the dish.

4 Add the oxtail, wine and stock, then add the thyme, bay leaf, sugar, tomato purée, lemon juice, salt and freshly ground black pepper.

5 Bring just to the boil, cover and put into the oven to braise for 4–5 hours, until tender.

6 When the meat is cooked and falls easily off the bone, remove the vegetables and meat from the pan with a slotted spoon. Put the meat in the fridge to chill and discard the vegetables but retain the sauce remaining.

7 Push the sauce through a sieve into a pan. Boil to reduce if necessary (it depends on how strong you want the sauce to be). Check the seasoning after reducing the sauce.

8 Remove the fat from the chilled oxtail and take the meat from the bones in chunky pieces.

9 Preheat the oven to 180°C/350°F/Gas mark 4.

10 Place the oxtail meat in six dariole moulds or ramekins, and spoon over a little of the sauce to moisten. Put in a roasting tin, filled with enough hot water to come three-quarters of the way up the sides of the moulds. Put the meat in the oven to heat through for 20 minutes.

▶

11 Meanwhile, fry the celeriac cubes in a little oil for about 5 minutes or more, until evenly browned.

12 To serve, place a mound of oxtail on to each plate, pour the sauce around, scatter around the celeriac and scatter over chopped parsley and chives. Serve with mashed potatoes (see page 137) and buttered cabbage or greens.

Tandoori Welsh-Lamb Chops

Five Nations Rugby Curry – Gerry Mansfield

serves fifteen

30 thin-cut Welsh lamb chops (thin-cut)

for the marinade

6 tspn red chilli powder

juice of 1 lemon

6 tspn ground cumin

4 tbspn garlic purée

4 tbspn ginger purée

500 ml/14 fl oz crème fraîche

salt and pepper

1 Mix the chilli powder and lemon juice together. Add the cumin, garlic and ginger and mix well. Stir in the crème fraîche until it resembles a thick batter, adding a little water, if necessary, if the crème fraîche is very thick. Pour the mixture over the chops and ensure they are fully coated. Season and leave to marinate for at least 3 hours (preferably overnight).

2 Barbecue the chops over charcoal, basting with the marinade, until tender and blackened around the edges (about 5 minutes on each side) or grill for 10–12 minutes, turning once.

2 Serve as part of a big spread of Gerry's other recipes listed in The Cooks section on page 178.

Haunch of Wild Boar Roasted with Herbs and Garlic, in a Red-Wine Sauce

Gourmet Night – Gordon Irvine

For Gordon, former Scottish shipyard worker, evey family holiday is a gastronomic tour. He has eaten wild boar in France and Austria, where it is easier to find than in Britain. Some British farmers are now starting to produce it, though, and it is available by mail order and in specialist shops. A good butcher should be able to order it for you. It is a dense, flavoursome meat, which Gordon describes as a cross between beef and pork.

serves six

2–3 small onions, quartered

2 large carrots, sliced

1 tbspn olive oil

1.3 kg/3½ lb from a haunch of wild boar

450 ml/¾ pint red wine

3 tbspn brandy

2–3 cloves of garlic, thinly sliced

chopped fresh herbs (small bunch of parsley, a few sprigs of thyme and rosemary, 6 sage leaves)

salt and freshly ground black pepper

1 Preheat the oven to 190°C/375°F/Gas mark 5.

2 Put the onions and carrots into a roasting tin or terracotta 'chicken brick'.

3 Heat the oil in a heavy frying-pan and brown the wild boar over a high heat on all sides until nicely coloured. Place the meat on top of the vegetables in the roasting tin or brick.

4 Pour off the fat from the frying-pan and add the wine, scraping up the residue from the meat. Bubble for a couple of minutes to burn off the alcohol (otherwise it may taste bitter). Add the brandy and either flame it (easily done if cooking on gas by tipping the pan towards the flame until it catches) or boil it for a further 2 or 3 minutes.

5 Sprinkle the meat with garlic and herbs. Season with salt and pepper. Cover with foil and place in the preheated oven for 1 hour 20 minutes. Adjust the time according to the size of the joint, allowing 20 minutes per 500 g/1 lb plus 20 minutes. Keep basting or turn the meat over in its juices, roughly every half hour. Like pork, wild boar should be well cooked.

▶

6 Twenty minutes before the end of the cooking time, remove the meat from the oven. Drain the juices into a bowl, separating off some (but not all) of the excess fat, and sieve the remaining juices into a pan. Put the meat back into the oven for a further 20 minutes, uncovered.

7 Take the meat out of the oven and rest, covered, for 10 minutes.

8 Boil the sauce to reduce it by roughly two-thirds to get a good, strong flavour. Check the seasoning and add more salt and pepper if needed.

9 Serve slices of wild boar with the reduced red-wine sauce, Puy lentils and French beans. Carrot bâtons, blanched and fried in olive oil in which you have begun to cook whole, unpeeled garlic cloves until nicely browned and tender (squash the pureéd flesh out of the skins and over the carrots), and creamy mashed potatoes, baked in ramekins with a large knob of butter on top, until browned and slightly puffed, are great accompaniments.

Curried Goat

Hampstead Callaloo – Bobby Gangar

serves twenty

5 kg/10 lb boneless goat meat, trimmed and cut in 2.5 cm/1 in chunks
juice of 2 limes or lemons (optional)
2 large onions, roughly chopped
2 tbspn HP Brown Sauce
1 tspn hot pepper sauce (or more if preferred)
1 tspn worcestershire sauce
1 tspn angostura bitters
1 tspn soy sauce
1 tspn cayenne pepper
1 tspn ground turmeric
½ 'scotch bonnet' pepper
salt and pepper
4 tbspn vegetable oil
6 heaped tbspn curry powder

for the green seasoning

1 bunch each of fresh parsley, thyme, chives and coriander
1 bulb of garlic, chopped or crushed
4 tbspn white-wine vinegar
4 tbspn water

to make the green seasoning

1 Roughly chop the herbs and blend until smooth with the chopped or crushed garlic, white-wine vinegar and water. Store in a screw-top jar for up to 1 month in the fridge.

to make the curry

1 Wash the meat in lime or lemon juice (optional) and then rinse in fresh water and place in a large bowl. Add the onions to the meat along with 4 tbspn of the green seasoning and all of the other ingredients except 3 tbspn of the curry powder and the vegetable oil. Marinate for at least 8 hours (or overnight).

2 Heat the oil in a large saucepan until it is beginning to smoke. Add the rest of the curry powder and fry for 30 seconds. Add the meat (along with the marinade). Stir well and cook on a low heat for 40 minutes or until tender. Stir occasionally and add a little water as necessary, to prevent it from burning. Serve with rice or roti.

Moussaka

Greco-Italian Surprise Party – Marina Schofield

serves twenty

3–4 large aubergines

2 kg Desiree potatoes

plain flour, seasoned, for coating

1.5 kg/3 lb minced lamb

2 large onions

1 bulb of garlic, chopped

2 tspn ground cinnamon

2 tbspn chopped fresh mint

1 tbspn chopped fresh oregano

3 tbspn tomato purée

oil, for frying

salt

for the sauce

120 g/4 oz unsalted butter

4 tbspn plain flour

1.2 litres/2 pints milk

grated nutmeg, salt and pepper

3 large eggs

Greek or parmesan or Emmental cheese

paprika

1 Slice and salt the aubergines and leave in a bowl for at least 1 hour. Par-boil the potatoes, drain, put in cold water and set aside. Preheat the oven to 190°C/ 350°F/Gas mark 4.

2 Rinse the aubergines and squeeze out the water. Sieve the flour into a plastic bag. Put a few aubergines in the bag at a time and shake until lightly floured.

3 In a frying-pan dry-fry the mince (no oil needed here). Add the onions, garlic, cinnamon, mint, oregano and tomato purée and cook through. If the mixture becomes dry, add a little water. Divide the meat mixture between two large ovenproof dishes.

4 In a clean frying-pan, fry the aubergines in the oil until golden brown. Layer the aubergines on top of the meat. Slice the potatoes quite thinly and fry them in a little oil. Add a little more tomato purée to give colour, if desired. Place the potatoes on top of the layer of aubergines.

to make the sauce

1 Melt the butter, add the flour and cook until lightly golden, gradually adding the milk until the sauce thickens, stirring all the time. Once thickened, remove from the heat and add nutmeg and salt and pepper. Cool slightly. Add the eggs to the sauce and whisk very quickly, until thoroughly blended. Pour the sauce over the layer of potatoes. Crumble the cheese on top, sprinkle with paprika and bake for 45 minutes.

to serve

1 Serve with warm crusty bread and a simple green salad.

Sweet and Sour Pork

Chinese Moon Festival – Rose Billaud

serves twenty

500 g/1 lb boneless pork
½ tspn salt
½ tspn ground pepper
2 tbspn plain flour
4 tbspn oil
1 onion, chopped
1 green pepper, seeded and chopped
1 red pepper, seeded and chopped
450 g/15 oz tin of pineapple chunks, including juice
2 tbspn cornflour, mixed with a little water

for the sauce

4 tbspn tomato ketchup
4 tbspn sugar
4 tbspn vinegar (white or malt, depending on taste)
2 tbspn light soy sauce
75 ml water

1 Chop the pork into small pieces. Put into a bowl and add salt, pepper and flour. Mix well.

2 Heat 1 tbspn of oil in a wok or pan. When hot, add the pork, piece by piece. Cook on both sides until brown and crisp. Set aside.

3 Mix all the sauce ingredients together.

4 Chop the vegetables and stir-fry them in 3 tbspn of oil, doing the onions first. Stir in the pineapple and juice.

5 Add the sauce. When boiling, add the pork. Thicken with the cornflour and stir until smooth and well blended. Serve with plain boiled rice or as part of a big spread of Rose's other recipes listed in The Cooks section on page 178.

Beef with Ceps

Mushroom Magic – Bob Wootton

serves eight

1.75 kg/3½ lb good beef fillet

brandy

900 ml/1½ pints veal stock

1 tbspn bramble jelly

sprig of winter savory

1 tspn Dijon mustard

1 tspn coriander seeds

500 g/1 lb fresh spinach

500 g/1 lb fresh ceps

3–4 tbspn olive oil, for frying

port, for deglazing

salt and pepper

1 Preheat the oven to 250°C/480°F/Gas mark 8. Prepare the beef for flash roasting by rubbing it with brandy and then browning it on all sides in a roasting pan on the hob.

2 Roast for 25 minutes or less, until the beef is brown and crisp on the outside but still very rare at the centre. Allow to rest for at least 10 minutes.

3 Heat the veal stock and add the bramble jelly, savory, Dijon mustard and coriander seeds. Reduce until you have a good coating consistency. Strain through a fine sieve and reserve.

4 Meanwhile, wash the spinach thoroughly and steam using only the water clinging to the leaves. When cooked, press all the water out of it (this is best done using the bottom of a bowl to compress the spinach in a round sieve). Keep the spinach warm.

5 Clean the ceps, removing the spongy spores, and chop into chunky pieces. Sauté in olive oil at a high heat, caramelizing the surface of the ceps without overcooking the insides. Put the ceps to one side. Deglaze the pan with a drop of port and add this juice to the reserved stock, to complete the sauce. Season the sauce with salt and pepper.

6 Assemble by placing a pile of steamed spinach in the centre of each plate, mounted by a tournedos-style slice of beef, surrounded and covered by pieces of cep and drizzled liberally with the sauce. Accompany with a small pool of very loose mashed potatoes, almost as a sauce.

Raised Pie

Tory Blues – Marguerite Vincent

serves ten

for the Pâte Moulée

300 g/10 oz plain flour

150 g/5 oz butter, chilled

2 eggs, beaten

1 tspn salt

4–6 tbspn water

for the filling

3 or 4 boneless, skinless
chicken thighs

3–4 turkey breasts,
cut in long strips

approximately 350 g/12 oz
lean gammon, cut in
julienne strips

salt and pepper

for the stuffing

250 g/8 oz white breadcrumbs

30 g/1 oz fresh parsley,
chopped

handful of chopped fresh thyme
(dried if not available)

lemon juice

1 clove of garlic, chopped

60 g/2 oz butter, softened

1 egg, beaten

1 Make the pastry: sift the flour into a bowl, cut in the butter, add 1 beaten egg and salt. Initially use only 3–4 tbspn of water, gradually adding a little more if necessary as you draw the mixture together with your hands. Roll the pastry into a ball and put in the refrigerator for 2 hours.

2 Preheat the oven to 180°C/350°F/Gas mark 4 and grease a long spring-loaded loaf tin, about 30 x 10 cm/12 x 4 in. Make the stuffing by combining the dry ingredients and rubbing in the lemon juice, garlic, butter and egg. Or blend together in a food processor if you have one.

3 Next, grease your tin well and line with baking parchment, also well greased. Cut off a third of the pastry and set aside for the top. Roll out the remainder and use it to line the tin.

4 Then take a small piece of stuffing, roll it into a ball and place in the middle of each boned chicken thigh; roll the ends over firmly.

5 Lay the turkey strips along the bottom of the pie, then position the stuffed chicken thighs on top, filling in the crevices with more of the stuffing mixture. Lastly arrange the gammon strips on top. This should create a colourful mosaic when the pie is cut.

6 Roll out the remaining third of pastry for the top. Cut into a lattice design and lay on top of the pie, brushing with beaten egg.

7 Bake for 1–1½ hours.

8 Allow to cool completely before turning out, to avoid the pastry coming away from the filling. Serve as part of a cold buffet spread, with a choice of salads.

Pickled Brisket

A Nice Bit of Brisket – Josie Livingstone

serves four

1.5–1.7 kg/3–3½ lb rolled pickled brisket

1 Boil the brisket for 2–2½ hours. Serve with Ayrshire potatoes, mashed with butter and a little milk, carrots cut into bâtons and cabbage cooked in 2 cups of the meat stock.

Gigot d'Agneau Cuit dans le Foin (Lamb in Hay)

Reg's Front Room Bistro – Reg Gray

Reg, who dreams of being Fred Astaire, is a man so misguided about his own talent, that his delusion is a talent in itself. His grand finale dance act to 'Simply the Best' by Tina Turner, was an unforgettable moment in the second series. This unusual lamb dish, adapted from a John Tovey recipe, was pretty memorable too.

serves six to eight

leg of lamb, at least 2.75 kg/6 lb

sea salt

120 g/4 oz butter, softened

2 tbspn chopped fresh herbs, e.g. basil, rosemary, parsley and mint

hay

1 Preheat the oven to 230°C/475°F/Gas mark 9. Rub the leg of lamb with salt and then coat with the butter. Sprinkle the chopped herbs over the joint to cover it evenly.

2 Put a layer of hay on to a trivet in a roasting dish, sit the meat on top of it and then pack more hay around the meat to cover it completely. Seal with foil and then cook for 30 minutes. Then reduce the heat to 200°C/400°F/Gas mark 6 and cook for a further 2 hours.

3 Allow the joint to sit for 15 minutes after removing it from the oven before taking off the hay and serving. Use the meat juices that have collected in the bottom of the dish to make a rich gravy.

Stuffed Pork en Croûte

Dinner with the Dawsons – Peggy Dawson

serves four

1 pork fillet (tenderloin)

juice of ½ lemon

salt and pepper

500 g/1 lb spinach, washed and trimmed

175 g/6 oz minced pork

1 tspn chopped fresh rosemary

120 g/4 oz mushrooms, chopped

120 g/4 oz shallots, chopped

¼ tspn grated nutmeg

1–2 tbspn oil

1 apple, peeled and cut in 1 cm/½ in chunks

fresh redcurrants

sprig each of sage, rosemary, bay and lemon balm

300 ml/½ pint apple juice

275 g/9 oz puff pastry

1 egg, beaten

1 Preheat the oven to 200°C/400°F/Gas mark 6.

2 Flatten the fillet into a thin rectangle, sprinkle with lemon juice and season with salt and pepper.

3 Cook the spinach in just the water clinging to the leaves after washing, for a few minutes. Squeeze out the spinach well and lay along the centre of the pork in an 8 cm/3 in wide strip. Mix the minced pork with some rosemary and put it on top of the spinach.

4 Sweat the mushrooms, shallots and nutmeg together in a little oil. Put on top of the minced pork. Scatter the chopped apple and a few redcurrants on top. Roll up the sides of the meat around the filling and, with some string, tie up the parcel tightly into a roll.

5 Place in a baking tray on a bed of sage, rosemary, bay, lemon balm and the apple juice and roast for 15 minutes. Lower the oven temperature to 180°C/350°F/Gas mark 4 and cook for a further 40 minutes.

6 Remove from the oven and leave until cool enough to handle. Reserve the juices for gravy.

7 Preheat the oven to 200°C/400°F/Gas mark 6. Roll the puff pastry into a rectangle much larger than the meat roll (reserving a little pastry for cutting out decorations). When the meat has cooled, wrap up the parcel in the pastry, wetting the edges and tucking these underneath. Score the top of the pastry. Decorate with pastry shapes, which you should brush with water to make them adhere. Paint the surface with an egg wash.

8 Place on a baking tray and bake for 15 minutes; then reduce the oven to 190°C/375°F/

▶

Gas mark 5 and cook for a further 45 minutes. This second cooking is the main one for the pork and it should be enough to cook the pork thoroughly.

9   Serve in slices, with redcurrant or apple sauce and a gravy made from the reserved juices from the meat.

Rack of Pork

The Feast of Samhain – Ozi Osmond

You need enough pork to be able to serve at least two chops to each guest. Ask your butcher to roll the racks so that the ribs are jutting out about 5 cm/2 in at the top.

serves eight

2 racks of pork

300 ml/½ pint red-wine vinegar

cloves (as many as you have chops)

olive oil

300 ml/½ pint cider

2 oranges

bay leaves (twice as many as you have chops)

10 unpeeled garlic cloves

2 onions, cut in chunks

salt and pepper

250 ml/8 fl oz mead (optional)

orange slices and bay leaves, to decorate

1   Preheat the oven to 200°C/400°F/Gas mark 6. Interlink the two racks of pork so they fit tightly together. Score the fat on top and carefully pour the red-wine vinegar over, allowing it to be absorbed into the fat where it is scored. Push a clove into the fat on each chop. Brush with a little olive oil and pour over half the cider.

2   Zest one of the oranges and sprinkle the zest over the pork. Place a bay leaf on each chop.

3   Put the garlic cloves around the pork in the roasting tin. Place the onions around the pork. Season well with salt and pepper.

4   Roast for 20 minutes at 240°C/450°F/Gas Mark 8 and then for 35 minutes/lb at 190°C/375°F/Gas Mark 5. Then if there is a lot of liquid pour a little off. Pour the rest of the cider and the mead, if using, over the pork and roast for a further half hour.

5   Remove from the oven and decorate with a slice of orange on each pork rib and a fresh bay leaf. Serve with the juices from the pan poured over and a selection of roasted root vegetables, such as potatoes, parsnips and carrots.

Ndole

A Cameroonian Feast – Grace Elone

Bitterleaf is a green leafy plant which grows, both wild and cultivated, all over West Africa. As the name suggests, it's quite unpalatable in it's raw state. Pre-washed bitterleaf can be purchased dried or frozen in good African food stores. If fresh bitterleaf is used, it must be boiled with limestone and washed thoroughly several times before being added to the dish. Alternatively, spinach can be used in place of the bitterleaf.

serves ten

500 g/1 lb dried salt cod

900 g/2 lb boneless mutton or lamb, cubed

1.75 litres/3 pints water

2 large onions, chopped

30 g/1 oz fresh root ginger, peeled and chopped

pinch of curry powder

3 beef stock cubes

1 fresh chilli

6 tbspn cooking oil

6 fresh tomatoes or 1 tin of peeled plum tomatoes, chopped

150 g/5 oz agussi (melon seeds) or pumpkin seeds

60 g/2 oz dried shrimps, ground

750 g/1½ lb bitterleaf or spinach

salt and pepper

1 Pre-cook the dried cod in the pressure cooker for 30 minutes (or boil in plenty of water for 2 hours).

2 Cook the cubed mutton or lamb in the water with 1 chopped onion, the chopped ginger, curry powder, beef stock cubes and the whole chilli for 45 minutes.

3 Fry the second chopped onion in the oil.

4 Drain the meat, reserving the cooking water, add to the hot oil and brown for 5 minutes. Add the chopped tomatoes and the cooked, drained cod and simmer for 30 minutes.

5 Grind the melon seeds until they are a fine powder and add to the reserved meat stock. Pour this into the meat mixture, stirring well. Also add the ground dried shrimps, and cook for 20 minutes longer.

6 Finally, add the bitterleaf, season with salt and pepper and leave to cook for a further 20 minutes before serving with Fried Plantains (see page 133).

Roast Kid

Ancient Greek Symposium – Dimitris Vassilliou

This is adapted from a recipe by Apicius, the Roman epicure, from a Roman cookery book. It is thought to be originally Greek as it specifies quantities, whereas quantities were very rarely mentioned in Roman recipes. A fermented fish sauce called garum was very popular in Roman cooking; Thai fish sauce is the nearest modern equivalent to this.

serves six

6.5 kg/13 lb kid

2 tbspn peppercorns

salt and pepper

olive oil, for basting

for the marinade

600 ml/1 pint milk

125 ml/4 fl oz clear honey

1 tbspn crushed peppercorns

½ tspn of asafoetida powder (optional)

olive oil, for basting

for the sauce

8 fresh dates, crushed

4 tbspn Thai fish sauce

375 ml/12 fl oz dry red wine

2 tbspn clear honey

4 tbspn virgin olive oil

cornflour, mixed with a little water

1 Mix all the ingredients for the marinade together. Pour over the meat and make sure the peppercorns are evenly spread all over. Leave to marinate for 8 hours or more, turning occasionally.

2 At the same time as making the marinade, soak the dates in the fish sauce and a little red wine. Leave to marinate overnight too.

3 Preheat the oven to 200°C/400°F/Gas mark 6. Remove the meat from the marinade. Pat dry, place in a roasting tin and brush with seasoned olive oil. Roast for 20 minutes per 450 g/1 lb plus 20 minutes, turning once halfway through.

4 When the meat is nearly ready, pound the dates to a pulp, transfer to saucepan and add the remaining red wine, and the honey and olive oil. Bring to the boil and reduce. Add a very little cornflour to thicken.

5 When the meat is cooked, remove it from the oven and allow it to rest for 10 minutes before carving it into thick slices. Serve with a little sauce on the side.

Breakfast Kebab

Empire Club Breakfast – Duncan Douglas

serves one

slice of black pudding

1 mushroom

unsmoked bacon, wrapped
around a prawn

Cumberland sausage

cherry tomato

smoked bacon,
wrapped around a scallop

1 mushroom

slice of Toulouse sausage

cherry tomato

slice of white pudding

oil, if necessary

1 Heat the grill to hot.

2 Thread all the ingredients on to a large skewer.
Grill for 5 minutes or so, turning once and
making sure the sausages are thoroughly
cooked. Brush with a little oil, if necessary,
during cooking, to prevent the mushrooms from
drying out.

3 Serve with Duncan's Kedgeree.

Sugo

Raising the Roof, Italian Style – Teresa Ibbotsen

*Teresa's Sugo is a real 'Italian mamma's' recipe, a contender for
'heartiest ever dish' on TV Dinners. The sauce is served with Spinach
and Ricotta Ravioli (see page 118) and the meat is served
separately, as another course.*

serves eight

for the stuffed beef shank

1 beef shank, boned

2 tbspn chopped fresh parsley

500 g/1 lb minced pork

6 rashers of bacon,
rinded and chopped

1 large tomato, chopped

1 Preheat the oven to 150°C/300°F/Gas mark 3.

2 To stuff the beef shank, mix all the ingredients for
the stuffing together. Put in the middle of the
beef. Tie with string (a butcher can do this for
you, if you give him the stuffing). To stuff the pork
shanks and trotters, slash the inside of the shank,
without piercing the skin, to allow the stuffing
flavours to be absorbed by the meat. Line with
the slices of bacon.

▶

3 cloves of garlic, chopped

½ small fresh red chilli

for the stuffed pork shanks and trotters

2 boned pork shanks with trotters attached

6 rashers of bacon

500 g/1 lb pork mince

120 g/4 oz breadcrumbs

120 g/4 oz pancetta, cubed

chopped fresh parsley

3 cloves of garlic, finely chopped

salt and freshly ground black pepper

for the stuffing

6 pork sausages

4 tbspn olive oil, for frying

1 red onion, finely chopped

1 celery leaf, roughly chopped

2 bay leaves

3–4 cloves of garlic, smashed

250 ml/8 fl oz red wine

handful of dried porcini mushrooms, soaked in boiling water

4 x 400 g/14 oz tins of chopped tomatoes

1 tube of tomato purée

2 handfuls of roughly chopped fresh parsley

salt and pepper

2 tspn pesto

3 Mix all the other ingredients together well. Put the stuffing into the centre of the shank.

4 Roll up the meat, holding the edges together with a skewer.

5 Fold the trotter under the shank and tie with string.

6 Sear the sausages and pork and beef parcels in olive oil, until well browned.

7 Turn the heat down and add the onion, celery leaf and bay leaves. Stir well. Add the garlic and allow to infuse. Add the red wine, with the soaked porcini mushrooms. Lastly, add the chopped tomatoes.

8 Cook slowly in the oven for 4 hours, until the meat is very tender.

9 Thicken with the tomato purée and cook for a further 10 minutes. Add a handful of the parsley and pesto and cook for 5 more minutes.

10 Remove all the meats and slice them thickly. Arrange on a large platter, pour over the sauce and sprinkle with the rest of the chopped parsley.

Beef Wellington

Pozzi's Pavlova – Marion Postma

serves eight

for the puff pastry:

250 g/8 oz plain flour

120 g/4 oz margarine

pinch of salt

½ tbspn lemon juice

150 ml/¼ pint iced water

120 g/4 oz butter,
cut into 16 pieces

for the filling:

800 g/1¾ lb fillet steak

1 large onion

350 g/12 oz mushrooms

butter for frying

175 g/6 oz good
home-made pâté

beaten egg, for brushing

for the sauce:

tin of beef consommé

small sherry glass of Madeira

to make the pastry

1 Mix the flour, the margarine, a pinch of salt and the lemon juice with the water in a bowl with your hands. Once the pastry has formed a ball, knead a bit and then chill for 15 minutes.

2 Roll the pastry out into a brick shape and, using a rolling pin, make three quick depressions widthwise. Then roll the brick shape out into an oblong roughly 4 cm/1½ in thick. Place four of the butter pieces on the pastry oblong, fold one third over to the centre and then the other third over that. Use the rolling pin to press the edges firmly and trap the air, and chill the pastry for 15 minutes.

3 Repeat the whole rolling and chilling process three times more and, finally, chill the pastry for at least 30 minutes or until ready to use. Preheat the oven to 190°C/375°F/Gas mark 5.

4 Meanwhile trim the meat and roast for 30 minutes, basting now and then with the juices. Remove from the oven and leave to cool. Turn the oven up to 230°C/450°F/Gas mark 8.

5 Chop the onions and mushrooms as finely as possible. Melt a little butter in a small saucepan, stir the onion in and cook for 5 minutes, then add the mushrooms and cook over a gentle heat for a further 15–20 minutes.

6 Take the pastry from the fridge and roll it out to a rectangle approximately 35 x 25 cm/ 14 x 10 in. Trim the edges (keeping the trimmings for decoration), then spread the pâté over the centre and top with half the mushroom and onion mixture. Place the fillet on top and the

▶

rest of the mixture on top of that, pat down into a good shape. Brush the edges of the pastry with beaten egg, and wrap the pastry like a parcel around the meat. Roll out the pastry trimmings to make decorations.

7 Place the whole lot on a baking sheet, brush all over with beaten egg (including any decorations you have added), and bake for a further 30 minutes.

8 Make up the sauce by heating the consommé and adding the Madeira and any meat juices left in the pan. Serve with the beef wellington, which should be cut in thick slices, with mashed or boiled potatoes and seasonal vegetables.

Marinated and Barbecued Lamb
Gorse Warrior's Barn Feast – Pigeon Biter

serves four

4 lamb chops or steaks

for the marinade
___
60 g/2 oz paprika
___
15 g/½ oz freshly ground black pepper
___
15 g/½ oz salt
___
6 cloves of garlic, finely chopped
___
2 tbspn lemon juice
___
100 ml/3½ fl oz olive oil

1 Mix the paprika in a large bowl with the garlic, lemon juice, salt and pepper and olive oil. Whisk together.

2 Put in the lamb, turn it well to coat it in the marinade and leave it for at least 2 hours, turning it occasionally.

3 Light the barbecue. Remove the lamb from the marinade and pat dry. Reserve the marinade.

4 Cook the lamb for 5–8 minutes on each side, basting occasionally with the marinade. Serve with salads and other barbecue meats.

Poultry and Game

Hare and Venison Pie
Gorse Warrior's Barn Feast – Pigeon Biter

serves ten

1.25 kg/3 lb shortcrust pastry

250 g/8 oz sausagemeat

5 tspn chopped fresh oregano

1.75 kg/3½ lb hare joints

1.75kg/3½ lb boneless casserole venison

2 kg/4 lb belly pork, cubed

olive oil

2 heaped tspn each grated nutmeg, ground ginger and paprika

2 large onions, chopped

500 g/1 lb mushrooms, sliced

red wine

meat stock

salt and pepper

milk, for glazing

1 Line a large roasting tin with shortcrust pastry, then spread out a layer of sausagemeat, mixed with 1 tspn of the oregano. Refrigerate.

2 Brown all meat to seal; first the hare, then the venison, with the belly pork, in olive oil, adding some of the remaining oregano and mixed spices to each batch. Keep aside in a large flameproof casserole dish.

3 Fry the onions and mushrooms in the same pan, add equal quantities of red wine and stock and deglaze. Add to the meat to cover. Season and cook for 2–2½ hours.

4 Allow to cool, then preheat the oven to 180°C/350°F/Gas mark 4. Bone the meat and add to the pastry base and pour in the sauce. Brush the sides with milk. Place pie raisers to prevent the pastry from sinking and then top with another layer of shortcrust pastry. Pinch the sides to form a seal.

5 Glaze the top of the pastry with milk. Bake for about an hour, or until the pastry is golden brown. Serve with boiled or mashed potatoes and seasonal greens (cabbage, broccoli or spinach).

Chicken with Tarragon

Late Starter – Wendy Ingham

This classic French dish can also be served cold (reduce the chicken stock by a half and not two-thirds).

serves six

2 chickens (preferably free-range and/or corn-fed), about 1 kg/2¼ lb each, cut into 16 pieces (or 16 breasts, thighs and legs)

salt and freshly ground black pepper

40 g/1½ oz butter

oil

bouquet garni (the usual parsley, thyme, celery stalk and bay leaf, plus tarragon stems)

100 ml/3½ fl oz white wine

500 ml/18 fl oz dark chicken stock (see note)

¼ tspn cold butter

½ –1 tbspn chopped fresh tarragon leaves

1 tomato, peeled, seeded and diced

1 Season the chicken with the salt and freshly ground black pepper.

2 Heat the butter and the oil in a large frying-pan or a wide casserole dish and brown the chicken all over.

3 Add the bouquet garni, cover the pan and cook for approximately 30–40 minutes (the breasts can be removed after 20 minutes). Lift the chicken out and keep warm.

4 Pour off the fat, add the white wine to the juices and scrapings in the pan and boil to reduce almost completely.

5 Add the stock and reduce by two-thirds (or by half if serving cold).

6 Strain the sauce and return it to the pan. Whisk in the cold butter, add the chopped tarragon leaves and the tomato and leave on a very low heat for a few minutes, just to warm through the ingredients and bring out their flavour.

7 To serve, spoon the sauce over the chicken. Serve with Gratin Dauphinois (see page 134) and green beans.

Note: A classic tarragon chicken can be made with veal stock. Wendy's friend Lemmy makes a rich dark-gold version of chicken stock as a substitute. Roast the chicken carcass until brown and blacken two onion halves, cut-side down, in a dry frying-pan. Keep the skins on. Make the chicken stock in the usual way.

Lena's Three-Bird Roast

Fowl Play – Lena Warboys

serves fourteen

5.5 kg/12 lb goose, fat
removed and boned, except legs

2.25 kg/5 lb chicken, boned
and skinned

1.05–1.25 kg/2½–3 lb mallard
duck, boned and skinned

for the apricot stuffing

1 small onion, finely chopped

25 g/1 oz butter

50 g/2 oz no-soak dried
apricots, chopped

50 g/2 oz breadcrumbs

for the sage and onion stuffing

1 medium onion, finely chopped

25 g/1 oz butter

3 fresh sage leaves,
finely chopped

50 g/2 oz breadcrumbs

for the chestnut stuffing

8 whole tinned chestnuts

1 goose liver

tin of unsweetened
chestnut purée

75 g/3 oz breadcrumbs

25 g/1 oz butter

salt and pepper

1 To make the apricot and the sage and onion stuffings, fry the onions in the butter and then stir in all the other ingredients and leave for at least 30 minutes, so that the flavours develop. Preheat the oven to 220°C/425°F/Gas mark 7.

2 To make the chestnut stuffing, chop the chestnuts and the goose liver, and mix with all the other ingredients.

3 Lay out the goose on a flat surface and spread with the chestnut stuffing. Then place the boned chicken on top, followed by the sage and onion stuffing, which should be spread over the areas of the bird where there is less meat. Then add the duck meat and the apricot stuffing in a similar way.

4 Sew up the birds with large stitches, using a large needle and thread, moulding the bird back into the shape of a goose as you go. Leaving the bones in the back legs helps to ensure the bird retains its shape.

5 When completely sewn up, turn over, put on a trivet and roast for one hour.

6 Reduce the oven to 180°C/350°F/Gas mark 4 and cook for a further 2–3 hours.

Note: Use the bones to make stock. Render the fat and skin in the oven and use the fat for roast vegetables such as potatoes.

Casseroled Pheasant with Kumquats

The Boys Shoot – Anthony Zahara

Adapted from a recipe in Classic Game Cookery *by Julia Drysdale (Macmillan).*

serves twelve

4 pheasant

120 g/4 oz butter

500 g/1 lb shallots

120 g/4 oz plain flour

450 ml/¾ pint red wine

grated zest and juice
of 2 oranges

20 kumquats, sliced

4 tbspn redcurrant jelly

2.25 litres/4 pints stock
(preferably goose stock)

bouquet garni
(bay leaf, thyme and rosemary)

salt and pepper

12 rashers of streaky bacon

1 tbspn chopped fresh parsley,
to garnish

1 Preheat the oven to 170°C/325°C/Gas mark 3. Brown the pheasant all over in hot butter in a flameproof casserole and remove from the pan. Sauté the whole shallots briskly in the butter until they are just beginning to turn brown, shaking the pan frequently. Remove from the pan.

2 Add enough of the flour to the pan to take up the remaining fat. Mix well, and then add the wine, orange juice and zest, sliced kumquats, redcurrant jelly and stock. Bring to the boil, stirring well.

3 Put the pheasant back into the dish and surround with the shallots. Tuck in the bouquet garni. Season with salt and pepper. Cover tightly and cook for 1–1½ hours.

4 When nearly cooked, roll up the bacon rashers, place on a baking tray and cook in a moderately hot oven (190°C/375°F/Gas mark 5) for 5–10 minutes, until slightly crisp. Add these to the casserole dish just before serving, check the seasoning and sprinkle with the freshly chopped parsley. Serve with saffron mashed potatoes and braised celery hearts or roasted red peppers and green beans.

Murgh Makhani (Butter Chicken)

The Karahi Club – Nina and Sumita Dhand

serves six

for the tikka marinade

1 tspn salt
3 dpsn natural yoghurt
juice of 1 lime/1 tbspn lemon juice
2 tspn garam masala
2 tspn red chilli powder
2 tspn coriander powder
2 tspn tandoori masala (ground coriander, ginger, cinnamon and nutmeg)
2 tspn kasoori methi or ground fenugreek
2 tspn chopped ginger
2 tspn chopped garlic
2–3 dspn vegetable oil
3–4 finely chopped green chillies
750 g/1½ lb boned chicken, cubed

to complete the makhani sauce

150 g/5 oz butter
2 tspn ground cumin
2 tspn tomato purée
4 tspn honey
150ml/5 fl oz double cream
3 tspn kasoori methi, crushed or ground fenugreek
1 tbspn lime juice
1 tspn black pepper

for the tomato sauce

(2x) 400 g/14 oz tins of tomatoes, puréed
1½ tspn fresh ginger purée
1½ tspn chopped fresh garlic purée
3 chopped green chillies
1 tspn kashmiri deghi mirch paprika
5 cloves
1 tspn salt
240 ml/8 fl oz water

1 Mix all the ingredients for the marinade together in a large bowl. Mix in the chicken pieces and leave in the fridge to marinate overnight.

2 Preheat the oven to 240°C/480°F/Gas mark 8. Put all the ingredients for the tomato sauce in a large pan, bring to the boil, reduce the heat and simmer for 20 minutes, until thick. Sieve the sauce and then leave to the side.

3 Meanwhile, transfer the chicken to a roasting tin, with its marinade, cover with foil and bake for 5 minutes. Then lower the heat to 200°C/400°F/Gas mark 6 and cook for 15–20 minutes.

4 In a pan, melt the butter and add the ground cumin. To this, add the tomato sauce. Leave to boil for a few minutes.

5 Add the tomato purée and the honey. Add the cream, kasoori methi, black pepper and lime juice and boil on a very gentle heat for a few minutes.

6 Finally, add the chicken tikka. Mix well and heat through. Serve with Tandoori Roti, Nan or rice.

Smoked Rabbit and Pheasant in a Wild Mushroom Gravy

Teepee Tea – Sam Thornley

Having opted out of the London rat-race, Sam Thornley took to living in a Teepee in the Scottish Lowlands. Most of his day was geared towards gathering and preparing food – something his guests at the Teepee soon came to appreciate. Sam frequently uses 'roadkill' rabbit and pheasant that he finds at the roadside. Roadkill should be as fresh as possible and not too squashed. Your nose is the best test of freshness. Give it a squeeze to check there is some meat on it. Remember, it is illegal to pick up something that you yourself have knocked down on the road.

serves six

2 rabbits, skinned and boned, bones reserved

1 pheasant, skinned and boned, bones reserved

3 small onions, chopped

5 cloves of garlic, crushed

olive oil

2 generous handfuls of dried mushrooms, e.g. field, parasol and cep

fresh thyme

red wine

fresh cream

chopped fresh parsley, to garnish

for the stock

1 onion, chopped

vegetable leaves

salt and pepper

1 Make a rich stock by adding water to the pheasant and rabbit bones, with a chopped onion, vegetable leaves and seasoning. Leave to bubble away on the fire or stove for at least a day.

2 Meanwhile, skewer the pieces of meat and hang them above the fire to smoke, preferably for two days. As the meat cures, it will darken to a rich, claret colour. If you don't have access to a fire, the recipe works just as well with unsmoked meat.

3 Soften the onions with the crushed garlic, in the oil over a gentle heat. Cut the meat up into bite-size pieces, add to the pan and brown for 5 minutes. Break in the dried mushrooms, and add lots of fresh thyme, enough of the stock to cover the meat and a generous dash of red wine. Leave to simmer until you have a rich, mushroomy gravy – about 20–30 minutes.

4 Just before serving, stir in a swirl of cream and garnish with chopped parsley.

Goose Kebabs, with Cranberry and Port Sauce

Christmas Tree – Tony Kitchell

serves six

*12 bay twigs, with leaves
removed and one end whittled
to a sharp point*

*2 goose breasts, cubed,
about 750 g/1½ lb, skinned*

500 g/1 lb prunes

24 bay leaves

for the marinade

600 ml/1 pint port

juice of 1 lemon

150 ml/¼ pint olive oil

*bunch of fresh parsley,
finely chopped*

salt and pepper

for the stock

1 goose carcass

olive oil

175 g/6 oz carrots, sliced

120 g/4 oz onions, sliced

120 g/4 oz celery, sliced

salt and pepper

3.5 litres/6¼ pints water

for the sauce

*250 g/8 oz shallots,
finely chopped*

2 tbspn olive oil

250 g/8 oz fresh cranberries

150 ml/¼ pint port

salt and pepper

1 Mix all the marinade ingredients together. Put in the cubed goose breasts and marinate overnight.

to make the stock

1 Preheat the oven to 180°C/350°F/Gas mark 4. Brown the goose carcass in a little olive oil in the oven. Add the carrots, onions and celery to the goose carcass. Season. Cover with foil and leave to sweat for 15 minutes. Add 150 ml/¼ pint of the water and reduce. Add the remaining water and simmer gently for several hours. Skim off any fat and strain.

to make the sauce

1 Sweat the chopped shallots in a little olive oil. Add the fresh cranberries (reserving a few for decoration). Cook until the cranberries are soft. Deglaze the pan with the port. Thin with a little goose stock and simmer gently. Take off the heat and allow to cool before blending in a liquidizer. When all the sauce is blended, sieve it and return to the heat. Thin with a little more goose stock, if necessary. Season to taste. Add the remaining cranberries for decoration – do not allow them to cook too much – they should remain whole.

to make the kebabs

1 Take the goose out of the marinade and carefully thread the cubes on to the bay twigs, interspersing the pieces with bay leaves and prunes.

2 Cook the kebabs on a hot barbecue. Be careful that no goose fat catches alight. Serve with the cranberry and port sauce, baked potatoes and some salads.

Duck with Lily Flowers and Chinese Mushrooms

Chinese Moon Festival – Rose Billaud

Lily flowers are an unusual ingredient, but can easily be found, dried, in oriental grocer's. They have a pleasant, smoky flavour, but this is still a great dish even if they are left out.

serves twenty

1 good-size duck

salt

2 tbspn dark soy sauce

1 tspn five-spice powder

2 tbspn soya oil

3 cloves of garlic, finely chopped

pinch of MSG (optional)

2 handfuls of dried Chinese mushrooms, soaked in warm water until soft, and drained

2 handfuls of dried lily flowers

3 tbspn light soy sauce

2 tspn sugar

for the dip

2 tspn sugar

2 tspn white vinegar

piece of fresh root ginger, peeled and cut in thin strips

1 Preheat the oven to 190°C/375°F/Gas mark 5. Rub the duck with salt, dark soy sauce and five-spice powder.

2 Place in the oven to cook for 40 minutes.

3 Remove from the oven, drain off the juices and leave the duck on a platter.

4 In a wok or big pot, heat the soya oil and stir-fry the garlic with a pinch of salt and a pinch of MSG.

5 Stir-fry the drained mushrooms and lily flowers, adding the duck juice, light soy sauce and sugar.

6 Add a cup of water and the duck. Braise for 20 minutes, until tender.

7 When cooked, remove the duck from the wok and chop into pieces. Arrange on a serving platter and pour over the sauce.

8 To make the dip, add the sugar and white vinegar to taste to the ginger, and mix well. Pour into a small dish and serve with the duck and some plain boiled rice.

Snipe and Woodcock à la Gourmande

In Search of Love – Simon Kelton

Eating the innards of both snipe and woodcock is a tradition revered by game aficionados, but the squeamish need not comply!

serves eight

8 snipe

8 woodcock

8 slices of bacon

120 g/4 oz butter

for the sauce

600 ml/1 pint red wine

8 tbspn port

120 g/4 oz pâté de foie gras

2 tbspn double cream

6 tbspn brandy

salt and pepper

2 tspn lemon juice

for the croûtons

8 heart-shaped slices
of brown bread

butter, for frying

1 Preheat the oven to 220°C/425°F/Gas mark 7. Pluck the birds and remove the gizzards. To do this, use a sharp knife tip to make a slit in the thin skin of the bird's abdomen, slightly to the right of centre. Insert a trussing needle and locate the hard lump of the gizzard. Pull it out and sever it from the rest of the innards. Next, skin the head by cutting around the neck and beak. You could ask your butcher to do this for you.

2 Place a strip of bacon on the woodcock, and half a strip on each of the snipe. Put in roasting tins, with the butter. Roast the snipe for 10 minutes and the woodcock for 20 minutes.

to make the sauce

1 Once roasted, remove the birds from the roasting pans. Pour in 4 tbspn brandy and set alight. Pour in the wine, add the port and reduce the sauce by half.

2 Blend the foie gras with the cream and 2 tbspn brandy to a smooth paste. Season with salt and pepper. Halve the mixture; set half aside to spread on to the heart-shaped croûtons. Remove the innards from the birds and sieve into the remaining paste. Add the lemon juice and stir the paste into the reduced sauce. Season with salt and pepper.

▶

to make the croûtons

1 Fry the croûtons in butter and then spread with the foie gras paste.

to serve

1 Place the birds on plates with the croûtons and serve with the sauce, seasonal greens such as kale or savoy cabbage, and game chips.

Rabbit Casserole
Run Rabbit Run – Hilary Waterhouse

serves ten

5 rabbits, jointed

175 g/6 oz flour, seasoned

120 ml/4 fl oz oil

120 g/4 oz butter

300 g/10 oz gammon, chopped

4 large carrots, diced

2 parsnips, diced

250 g/8 oz mushrooms, sliced

4 red onions, chopped

1 large unpeeled, cox's apple, cored and diced

1.5 litres/2½ pints dry cider

1 tbspn rosemary and apple jelly

2 tspn Dijon mustard

4 juniper berries, crushed

1 tbspn chopped fresh herbs, e.g. rosemary, sage and thyme

salt and pepper

1 Preheat the oven to 180°C/350°F/Gas mark 4. Dry the rabbit pieces and chop into small pieces. Coat the rabbit pieces in seasoned flour by shaking them in a polythene bag until well coated. Continue in batches until all are done.

2 Melt the oil and butter in a large flameproof casserole dish. Fry the rabbit pieces to brown and seal. Add the gammon and gently fry. Add the vegetables and apple. Let all fry for a few minutes.

3 Pour in enough cider to cover; stir in the rosemary and apple jelly, mustard, juniper berries and herbs. Season to taste, cover the pan and bring to boil on top of the stove. Then cook at the top of the oven for 30 minutes. Turn the oven down to 150°C/300°F/Gas mark 2 and cook for about another 1–1½ hours. Remove the bones before serving, if preferred. Gratin Dauphinois (see page 134) is a very good accompaniment.

Venison Glen Loth

The Laird's Supper – Michael Dudgeon

serves eight

1.5 kg/3 lb boned saddle of venison

about 500 g/1 lb flour

salt and pepper

butter and olive oil, for frying

½ bottle of red wine

300 ml/½ pint single cream

1 Cut the venison into 2.5 cm/1 in thick slices.
2 Season the flour with salt and pepper.
3 Put the flour on to a board and hammer it into the venison slices with a steak tenderizing hammer, so they end up as thin as possible.
4 Heat the butter and oil in a frying-pan, and fry the venison slices gently in batches, removing them from the pan when ready and keeping them warm.
5 Deglaze the frying-pan with the red wine and simmer until reduced. Add the cream and cook until smooth. Season to taste with salt and pepper.
6 Serve the venison with sauce poured over the venison slices. Mashed potatoes or Gratin Dauphinois (see pages 137 and 134) and seasonal greens are a good accompaniment.

Peking Duck

All Over the Pacific – Penny Sinclair

serves six

2 tbspn honey

1 duck

to serve

2 bunches of spring onions, finely chopped

1 medium-size cucumber, finely chopped

hoisin sauce

Chinese pancakes

1 Melt the honey in a cup of hot water.
2 In a sink, scald the duck with boiling water to tighten the skin. Shake off the excess water and carefully cover the duck with the mixture of honey and water. Make sure that every part of the skin is covered.
3 When the duck is thoroughly covered, hang it up to dry using two butcher's hooks under the wings. It should be left to dry for as long as possible – 12 hours minimum. The skin will become like parchment.

▶

4 Pre-heat the oven to 180°C/350°F/Gas mark 4. Place the duck in the middle of the oven straight on the oven rack, breast-side up. Cook for 20 minutes. Turn the duck over and cook for a further 30 minutes. Turn the duck over so it is breast-side up again and cook for a final 20 minutes. Adjust the oven, depending on the intensity of colour of duck skin: it should be a fairly dark red.

5 Serve with finely chopped spring onions and cucumber, hoisin sauce and some steamed Chinese pancakes.

Baked Jerk Duck

A Jamaican Farewell – Paige Mulroy

serves six

6 duck legs

for the jerk rub

1 onion, chopped

2 tbspn chopped fresh thyme

2 tspn ground
Jamaican pimento

½ tspn ground cinnamon

whole garlic, sliced

about 6 spring onions, chopped

2 tspn salt

1 tspn black pepper

1 tspn nutmeg

1 hot 'scotch bonnet' chilli

125 ml/4 fl oz olive oil

1 Combine all the 'jerk' ingredients into a paste.

2 Rub the paste into the duck legs and allow to marinate overnight.

3 Next day, preheat the oven to 180°C/350°F/ Gas mark 4 and bake the duck legs for 2 hours. Serve with Rice and Peas (see page 129) and Fried Plantain (page 133).

Chicken Fajitas with Tortillas

Scouts Honour – Niamh Watmore

serves six

3 onions

2 chillies

2 garlic cloves, crushed

1 tbspn chopped fresh coriander

grated zest and juice of 2 limes

6 chicken breast fillets

8 mixed coloured peppers

1 tbspn olive oil

salt and pepper

fresh coriander leaves,
to garnish

1 Cut the onions into wedges; slice the chillies.
2 Put the onions, chillies, garlic, coriander and lime zest and juice into a shallow dish and mix. Cut the chicken into pieces and leave to marinate overnight.
3 Cut the peppers into wedges.
4 Heat the oil in a pan. Remove the chicken and onions from the marinade. Add to the pan and cook on high heat, until brown. Remove the chicken from the pan.
5 Add the peppers to the onions in the pan and cook for 5 minutes.
6 Return the chicken to the pan, with the marinade. Cook for about 5 minutes, until the chicken is cooked.
7 Season the chicken with salt and pepper and sprinkle with coriander leaves.

for the tortillas

300 g/10 oz plain white flour

pinch of salt

50 g/2 oz white vegetable fat

175 ml/6 fl oz warm water

to make the tortillas

1 Mix the flour, salt and fat together to resemble breadcrumbs.
2 Add warm water, to make a fairly warm dough.
3 Knead briefly; then divide into 12 pieces.
4 Roll out each piece into an 18 cm/6 in circle.
5 Cook the tortillas on a griddle pan for 1 minute on each side and serve with the chicken.

Moroccan Chicken Parcels

Road to Morocco – Howard Morgan

The technique of spraying the pastry is what gives these Moroccan pasties their characteristic golden glaze. Howard, a stickler for authenticity, tracked down the recipe, but you could, as an alternative, simply brush them with beaten egg before baking. If you cannot find evaporated goat's milk, ordinary tinned evaporated milk is a good alternative.

serves eight

for the pastry

150 g/5 oz chicken fat, chilled

300 g/10 oz plain flour, chilled

pinch each of ground cinnamon, ginger and grated nutmeg

pinch of salt

full-fat milk, if necessary

for the chicken

about 30 stoned dates

½ tspn ground cinnamon

4 cloves of garlic, chopped

1 small onion, chopped

8 chicken breasts

for the pastry spray

goat's milk (evaporated)

vegetable oil

beaten egg

paprika and white pepper, for dusting

1 Preheat the oven to 230°C/450°F/Gas mark 8. Put the chilled fat and flour in a bowl. Add a pinch each of cinnamon, ginger and nutmeg. Season. Pound the flour, fat and salt – try not to add water as this will make the pastry very hard when baked; add a very little full-fat milk if needed, to make a dough.

2 Purée the stoned dates, cinnamon, garlic and onion to a paste and spread on the chicken breasts.

3 Roll out enough pastry to cover the chicken with a very thin layer. Place a breast on the pastry and seal the 'envelope' with water and pinch the edges with your fingers or a fork. Repeat with the other breasts.

4 Arrange on a greased baking sheet and bake for 15 minutes.

5 Remove and spray with the pastry spray mixture, using a clean pastry mister. Do not use a brush as it will tear the pastry. After spraying, dust with paprika and white pepper and return to the hot oven for 5 minutes.

Pasta and Rice

Valençian Paella
Valencian Paella Party – Dave Hayward

As a gesture of authenticity, Dave has live snails from Valencia flown in for his paella parties, but you don't have to go to such extreme lengths. You can buy precooked snails tinned, frozen or vac-packed in many good delis and specialist food stores.

Or you can collect your own English garden snails, which, although they may not have had the benefit of Valencian sunshine and a wild rosemary diet, are exactly the same species as those Dave uses (what the French call petit gris). Collected snails should be kept in a box in a cool dark place and fed for at least three days on a one-item purgative diet: carrots, lettuce or rosemary. Or, if you really don't like snails, just add plain rosemary to get some of the flavour of the rosemary-fed snails! The Spanish like to serve their snails with the bodies out of the shell (though still attached), so they don't have to delve for them with pins. To achieve this, they put all the snails in a pan of cold water so that they come out of their shells. They then put them on a very low heat (with salt rubbed around the edge to deter any attempted escapes) and, as the temperature rises, they eventually 'fall asleep'. They are brought to the boil and then gently simmered for ten minutes until tender, at which point they are ready for further cooking – that is, they can be added to a paella or sautéed in very garlicky butter.

The quantities below are designed for Dave's 60 cm/24 in paella pan so, if you don't have one, you will need an extra-large frying-pan or a very wide saucepan. If you are brave, you could attempt to cook two half-size paellas in two separate frying-pans. Or use half the *ingredients for a smaller paella, to feed four. Dave has made his own customized paella barbecue but a well stoked conventional barbecue will produce sufficient heat for you to cook yours out of doors.*

serves eight

2 tbspn olive oil

250 g/8 oz chicken pieces, in 2-bite chunks

250 g/8 oz boneless rabbit, in 2-bite chunks

250 g/8 oz boneless duck, in 2-bite chunks

250 g/8 oz runner beans or long green beans, cut into 5 cm/2 in slices

½ green pepper, seeded and finely chopped

½ red pepper, seeded and finely chopped

1 large tomato, grated or skinned and chopped

1 clove of garlic, finely chopped

1 tspn paprika

200 g/7 oz butter beans, soaked overnight

500 g/1 lb long-grain rice

1–2 pinches of saffron

salt

15–20 snails, prepared as on page 112 (or tinned or vac-packed)

chopped fresh rosemary (optional)

1 Heat the oil in the pan and add all the meat. Fry, turning regularly, for 5 or 10 minutes, until all the pieces are nicely browned.

2 Add the runner/green beans and stir-fry for a couple of minutes.

3 Add the peppers and stir-fry for a couple of minutes.

4 Add the tomato and garlic and fry for 5 minutes, stirring occasionally.

5 Add the paprika and stir into the mixture, to heighten the colour and season the dish.

6 Pour on enough cold water to cover the meat and vegetables. (In a paella pan, the tradition is to add water until it comes up to the rivets of the pan.) Ideally, the water should be hard, like the water of Valença, so the water in Kent, where Dave lives, is fine. Simmer for 5 minutes.

7 Add the soaked butter beans and simmer for 10 minutes.

8 Add the rice. In Spain, the rice is poured across the paella pan in the shape of a cross. You have enough when it stands a finger higher than the liquid. Dave has found that a full pint glass just happens to hold the right amount for his pan.

9 Add enough saffron to give the paella a golden hue. Season with plenty of salt.

10 Add the blanched snails, still in their shells and/or a little extra rosemary.

11 Cook, without stirring, until the liquid has boiled away, controlling the heat and repositioning the pan so the paella bubbles evenly. Check the seasoning: an undersalted paella may taste bland. Don't worry if the rice starts to stick to the

▶

bottom of the pan as it's meant to – the crisp scrapings from the bottom, known as socarrat, are something the guests will fight over!

12 Hand out forks to the guests so that they can eat straight from the paella dish. Alternatively, serve on plates, trying to be fair with the snails and the socarrat.

Lobster Ravioli

A Literary Dinner – Lorna Macleod
(Based on a recipe from Le Manoir aux Quat' Saisons, *Raymond Blanc, Guild Publishing 1988)*

serves twelve

7 litres/8¾ pints water
45 g/1½ fl oz salt
2 live lobsters
melted butter, to serve

to prepare the lobster

1 Preheat the oven to 180°C/350°F/Gas mark 4.

2 In a large saucepan, bring 7 litres/8¾ pints of water to the boil with 45 g/1½ oz of salt (the amount of salt is very important – too much and all the juices are leached out; too little and the meat won't set properly). Kill the lobsters with a heavy blow from a sharp knife to the base of their heads. Then plunge into the boiling water for 10 seconds. Refresh in cold water and then drain. (An alternative method of killing the lobsters is to plunge them into a large saucepan of fast-boiling water, head first, ensuring they are completely immersed. Hold them under water with wooden spoons for two minutes.)

3 Open up the lobsters with scissors. Remove the intestine from the back of the lobster and throw away. Get out as much meat as possible from the back and the claws, reserving the shells for the stock. Scoop out the dark-green coral and reserve. Scrape out the blood (ink coloured) inside the head and reserve. Chop the legs and shells with a sharp knife or cleaver.

▶

for the mousse

1 tspn salt

1–2 tbspn olive oil, for frying

pinch of cayenne pepper

2 medium egg whites

400 ml/14 fl oz whipping cream

for the stock

200 g/7 oz onions, finely chopped

outer leaves of two fennel bulbs, finely chopped

1 stalk of celery, finely chopped

2 cloves of garlic, finely chopped

2 tbspn olive oil

7 medium tomatoes, finely chopped

sprig of fresh thyme

4 tbspn Cognac

200 ml/7 fl oz dry white wine

1.5 litres/2½ pints water

sprig of fresh tarragon, finely shredded

4 tbspn whipping cream

75 g/3 oz unsalted butter, chilled and cubed

salt and pepper

to make the mousse

1 Dice about 130 g/4½ oz of the lobster flesh, season lightly and fry in olive oil for a minute. Set aside.

2 Mix the remaining flesh with the blood, a pinch of cayenne, salt and the egg whites. Blend in a food mixer. When thoroughly mixed, push through a sieve. Then refrigerate for at least half an hour.

3 When the mixture is thoroughly chilled, remove from the fridge and slowly add 300 ml/½ pint of the cream. Mix gently to start with and then beat vigorously with a balloon whisk, incorporating as much air as possible. Add the rest of the cream, if necessary, depending on the texture and flavour.

4 Add the cooked lobster meat. Refrigerate.

to make the stock

1 Chop the onions, fennel, celery and garlic. Sweat in some of the olive oil for a few minutes. Add the tomatoes and thyme and allow to cook for a few more minutes.

2 In a separate pan, sweat the lobster shells in the rest of the hot oil for 2–3 minutes. Pour off the oil and deglaze the pan with cognac. Add the wine and boil for a few seconds; then add the cooked vegetables. Add the water and simmer for 30 minutes.

3 Add the tarragon and cook for a few more minutes.

4 Sieve the stock and then reserve half the liquid and reduce the rest to make about 3 tbspn of concentrated lobster stock. When this has cooled slowly, add to the mousse.

▶

for the pasta
250 g/8 oz strong white flour
5 egg yolks
2 pinches of salt
2 tbspn olive oil
1–2 tbspn water

for the pasta

1 Put all the ingredients in a food mixer and mix for about 30 seconds, or until the ingredients are just blended. Knead the dough thoroughly until smooth. Wrap in cling film and refrigerate for half an hour.

2 When chilled, divide the dough into four and put it through the pasta machine, starting on the widest setting and gradually working down to the thinnest (if you don't have a pasta machine, roll the pasta on a floured surface, with a floured rolling pin, as thinly as possible). Refrigerate once again.

constructing the ravioli

1 On a lightly floured surface, lay out the dough and cut into 7 cm/2¾ in rounds with a pastry cutter. Stretch out the rounds as thinly as possible and brush the edges with water. Place 1 tspn of the mousse on one half of each round and close them, to make half-moon shapes. Press the edges firmly to seal and place on a tray. Freeze for at least an hour.

to make the lobster sauce

1 Reduce the remaining lobster stock by a third. Stir in the cream and whisk in the cubed butter, a piece at a time. Season to taste.

to serve

1 Poach the frozen ravioli in boiling water for a minute. Reduce the heat and simmer for 5 minutes. Remove from the water and drain on a clean tea-towel. Place in a serving dish and brush with a little melted butter. Pour over the lobster sauce and serve.

Leah's Lasagne

Teen Girls Sleepover – Leah Scott

Once an exotic dish on the seventies dinner party circuit, Lasagne is now one of the first things a novice cook is likely to attempt. That was the case for 14-year-old Leah and a very precocious little Lasagne it was too!

serves eight

butter for frying

1 large onion, chopped

½ green, ½ red, ½ yellow pepper, seeded and chopped

120 g/4 oz mushrooms, sliced

750 g/1½ lb minced beef

2 x 400 g/14 oz tins of chopped tomatoes

½ tspn dried mixed herbs

salt and pepper

500 g/1 lb no-precook lasagne

for the sauce

500 ml/16 fl oz milk

45 g/1½ oz butter

45 g/1½ oz plain flour

salt and pepper

250 g/8 oz Cheddar cheese, grated

1 Preheat the oven to 180°C/350°F/Gas mark 4. Heat a frying-pan and melt a knob of butter. Add the onions, peppers and mushrooms and fry until soft.

2 Add the mince, gently breaking it up and turning it in the pan, until it is thoroughly browned.

3 Stir in the chopped tomatoes and dried herbs. Put the lid half on, and leave to simmer gently for about half an hour. Season to taste with salt and pepper.

to make the sauce

1 Heat the milk and set it aside. Melt the butter over a low heat, adding the flour and stirring together until you have a roux.

2 Slowly add the milk to the roux, until the mixture is thick and smooth. Season to taste with salt and pepper.

3 Assemble the lasagne by layering the mince mixture with sheets of lasagne and white sauce, ending with a layer of white sauce.

4 Sprinkle the cheese over the top.

5 Bake for 30–40 minutes, until the cheese is golden brown. Serve with a crisp green salad.

Spinach and Ricotta Ravioli

Raising the Roof, Italian-style – Teresa Ibbotsen

serves twelve

for the pasta

500 g/1 lb strong white flour

pinch of salt

5 eggs

for the ricotta cheese

2.25 litres/4 pints creamy milk

pinch of salt

8 tspn rennet (available from specialist food stores or chemists)

for the ravioli filling

500 g/1 lb fresh spinach, washed and trimmed

120 g/4 oz fresh white breadcrumbs

pinch of grated nutmeg

pinch of salt

1 egg

175 g/6 oz Parmesan cheese, grated

500 g/1 lb ricotta cheese, preferably home-made, crumbled

1 Make a well out of the flour and salt, crack the eggs into the well and mix with the hands into a big ball of dough, adding a very little water, if necessary. Roll into a sausage and cover with cling film as you work.

2 Roll out the dough in strips about 10 cm/4 in wide and 1–2 mm thick.

to make the ricotta cheese

1 Scald a saucepan with boiling water, to ensure it is clean and sterilized.

2 Bring the milk and salt to blood heat. Gently stir in the rennet and, as soon as the rennet starts to work, remove from the heat.

3 Leave to settle; after about 10 minutes the curds should be at the top and the whey at the bottom.

4 Skim off the curds with a slotted spoon and spoon into a cheesecloth (a clean piece of muslin).

5 Tie and hang up; leave to drip for 2–3 hours.

to make the filling

1 Steam the spinach in just the water clinging to the leaves after washing. Drain and chop finely. Squeeze out any liquid with your hands and allow to cool.

2 Add the breadcrumbs, nutmeg, salt, egg, parmesan and ricotta.

3 Mix with your hands, cover and leave to stand for 30 minutes.

4 Put small spoonfuls of filling on the sheets, brush with water round the edges and cover with another sheet of pasta.

5 Use a ravioli stamp or a wheeled pasta cutter to cut out the ravioli.

Kedgeree

Empire Club Breakfast – Duncan Douglas

serves six

6 eggs, to garnish

250 g/8 oz smoked haddock

450 ml/¾ pint milk

1 onion, chopped

1 carrot, chopped

1 bay leaf

6 peppercorns, crushed

175 g/6 oz smoked mackerel

15 g/½ oz butter, plus extra for serving

olive oil

1 green and 1 red pepper, seeded and chopped

2 leeks, chopped

250 g/8 oz arborio risotto rice

2 tspn paprika

salt and pepper

1 Lightly boil the eggs. Plunge immediately into cold water and leave to cool. When cool enough to handle, shell carefully and slice.

2 In a saucepan, put the smoked haddock and the milk, with the onion, carrot, bay leaf and crushed peppercorns. Bring to the boil and simmer for 10 minutes.

3 Strain, reserving the liquid. Make up to 450 ml/¾ pint with more warm milk. Keep hot.

4 Flake the haddock and skin and flake the smoked mackerel. Put aside.

5 Melt the butter with a little olive oil in a large, heavy-based pan. Fry the peppers for 2 minutes. Add the leeks and fry for a further 2 minutes. Add the rice to the mixture, coat the rice well and fry for 4 minutes.

6 Gradually, add the liquid from the poached fish 150 ml/¼ pint at a time. Gently stir until the liquid is absorbed and the rice is nice and creamy but still slightly *al dente* in texture. Add a large knob of butter, the paprika and salt and pepper to taste. Stir in the fish gently and heat through.

7 Spoon the kedgeree on to heated plates and top with slices of lightly boiled egg. Serve with Duncan's Breakfast Kebabs.

Pasticcio

Just Like Mamma made – Nicky Samengo-Turner

serves eight

3 tbspn light oil, for frying

dash of red wine

1.75 litres/3 pints rich tomato sauce (home-made if possible)

for the meatballs

500 g/1 lb minced beef

500 g/1 lb minced pork

500 g/1 lb minced veal

2 eggs, beaten

handful of finely chopped fresh basil and parsley

3 tbspn olive oil

½ yellow pepper, seeded and finely chopped

½ onion, finely minced

3 cloves of garlic, finely chopped

50 g/2 oz Parmesan cheese, grated

dash of Tabasco sauce

dash of lemon juice

pinch of chopped fresh oregano

salt and pepper

for the béchamel sauce

120 g/4 oz butter

75 g/3 oz plain flour

1.2 litres/2 pints milk

pinch of grated nutmeg

salt and pepper

to make the meatballs

1 Preheat the oven to 180°C/350°F/Gas mark 4. Combine all the ingredients for the meatballs and mix thoroughly. Roll the mixture into thumbnail-size meatballs.

2 In a frying-pan, heat the oil and fry the meatballs until nicely browned. Remove them from the pan and deglaze the pan with the red wine. Scrape up all the frying residue and tip the whole lot into the tomato sauce.

to make the béchamel sauce

1 Melt the butter in a heavy-based saucepan. Remove from the heat and sift the flour in, stirring constantly. Return the pan to the heat and gradually add the milk, a little at a time, stirring constantly. When all the milk has been added, turn the heat down and allow to cook for 5–10 minutes. Season with a little grated nutmeg and salt and pepper.

to assemble the pasticcio

1 Par-cook the pasta in a large saucepan of salted, boiling water. Drain and mix with the béchamel sauce.

2 Butter a large casserole dish and then combine the pasta, tomato sauce, ricotta, meatballs, mozzarella, parmesan and basil in alternating layers. As a topping, add a final layer of sliced mozzarella and more grated parmesan.

3 Bake, covered, for 30 minutes. Remove the lid and cook for a further 10 minutes, to brown the top. Serve with a green salad.

▶

additional ingredients

butter, for greasing
900 g/2 lb penne or 'unbroken' (longer, straighter) macaroni
375 g/12 oz ricotta cheese
3 buffalo mozzarella cheeses
375 g/12 oz good fresh Parmesan cheese, grated
fresh basil leaves

Curried Cannelloni
Old Girls Reunion – Heather Matuozzo

serves four

for the pancakes

120 g/4 oz plain flour, sifted
salt and pepper
2 eggs, beaten
600 ml/1 pint milk
1 tbspn chopped fresh coriander
1 tbspn grated fresh Parmesan cheese

for the filling

3 tbspn olive oil
2 cloves of garlic, finely chopped
500 g/1 lb mushrooms, chopped
8 tspn tikka masala paste
1 kg/2 lb frozen leaf spinach
2 tbspn sherry

to make the pancakes

1 Make the pancakes by sifting the flour and seasoning, adding the eggs and milk and whisking until smooth. Stir in the coriander and parmesan. Make up eight pancakes as usual and stack with greaseproof paper in between.

to make the filling

1 Preheat the oven to 200°C/400°F/Gas mark 6. In a large frying-pan, put the oil, garlic, mushrooms and tikka paste and fry for 2 minutes. Add the frozen spinach (still frozen, so it has not gone mushy), stir for 2–3 minutes and then add the sherry. Stir until the spinach is cooked and the sherry absorbed. Leave the mixture to cool.

2 Add the ricotta and mozzarella. Season. Put equal amounts of mixture in each pancake and roll up, cutting the edges to make them neat. Put into a greased ovenproof dish.

▶

500 g/1 lb ricotta cheese,
crumbled

500 g/1 lb mozzarella cheese,
cubed

salt and pepper

for the sauce

¼–1 fresh chilli, chopped

2 tbspn olive oil

500 ml/16 fl oz tomato passata

1½ tbspn chopped fresh
coriander

salt and pepper

2–3 tbspn grated Parmesan
cheese, to finish

for the raita sauce

150 ml/¼ pint live
natural yoghurt

2 sprigs of fresh mint

½ tspn chilli powder

to make the sauce

1 In a thick-bottomed pan, lightly fry the chillies to flavour the oil. Pour the passata tomatoes into the pan and cook for 15–20 minutes, to reduce. Add the coriander and season to taste. Pour the sauce over the cannelloni and sprinkle with parmesan. Bake for 20–25 minutes, or until the cheese has melted.

to make the raita sauce

1 Mix the ingredients together. Serve the sauce with the cannelloni.

Vegetarian

Vegetable Tower Provençale
Leaving Liverpool – Jon Ashton

serves four

2 aubergines

4 beef tomatoes

extra-virgin olive oil

salt

250 g/8 oz mozzarella cheese

for the sauce

2 tbspn olive oil

2 shallots, chopped

2 cloves of garlic,
finely chopped

torn fresh basil leaves to taste

2 courgettes, chopped

1 green pepper,
seeded and chopped

250 g/8 oz plum tomatoes,
puréed

300 ml/½ pint stock

salt and pepper

to make the sauce

1 Heat the oil and fry the shallots, garlic and basil. Add the chopped vegetables, puréed tomatoes and stock. Bring to the boil and reduce to a good pouring consistency. Season to taste with salt and pepper.

to make the towers

1 Heat the grill to hot. Slice the aubergines and tomatoes fairly thinly. Drizzle oil and salt over the aubergines and place under a hot grill.

2 Remove when golden and place four slices on a greased baking tray. Place a thin slice of mozzarella on top and build towers, alternating cheese, tomatoes and aubergines. Serve with the sauce.

Koki

A Cameroonian Feast – Grace Elone

Check out a West-Indian food store for cocoa leaves, palm oil, plantains and plantain string.

400 g/14 oz haricot beans, soaked overnight and drained
1 small fresh chilli, seeded and chopped
300 ml/½ pint palm oil
250 g/8 oz fresh spinach or cocoa leaves, chopped
6 fresh plantain leaves
salt

1 Wash the beans well and remove the skins. Pound them in a mortar (or grind in a blender or food processor), with the chilli and a bit of salt, until you have a smooth paste. Mix in the palm oil and the chopped spinach or cocoa leaves and a bit of water to make the mixture slightly liquid.

2 Press each plantain leaf in turn into a bowl, to make a well shape. Put some of the bean mixture into the leaf, gather the top of the leaf together and tie with plantain string. (Alternatively, the koki can be cooked in foil parcels.)

3 Steam in a covered pan with a little boiling water at the bottom for 1½–2 hours.

4 Before serving, untie the leaves and cut the koki into slices, like a cake. Serve with Fried Plantains (see page 133) and yam.

Sweet Baby Soul Burgers with Hot Corn Relish

Seventies Night – Monica Curtain and Sue Smallwood

serves fifteen
500 g/1 lb black-eyed beans, soaked overnight, drained and rinsed
2 large carrots, grated
120 g/4 oz mushrooms, chopped

1 Cook the black-eyed beans in plenty of fresh, boiling water, for 45–50 minutes, until completely soft.

2 Mash up the black-eyed beans. Mix together the carrots, mushrooms, chillies, ginger, garlic, onion, thyme, paprika, piri-piri and flat-leaf parsley. Beat one egg and mix well into the mixture.

▶

1 small fresh red chilli, seeded and chopped

1 small fresh green chilli, seeded and chopped

1 tspn grated fresh root ginger

2 cloves of garlic, finely chopped

1 large onion, finely chopped

1 tspn chopped fresh thyme

pinch of paprika

1 tspn piri-piri sauce (see page 25) or your favourite chilli sauce

small bunch of flat-leaf parsley, finely chopped

3 eggs

plain flour, seasoned and sifted, for coating

sunflower oil, for shallow-frying

salt and pepper

for the relish

4 corn on the cobs

salt and pepper

1 large red pepper, seeded and chopped

2 fresh red chillies, seeded and chopped

2 fresh green chillies, seeded and chopped

handful of chopped fresh marjoram

450 ml/¾ pint vegetable stock

250 g/8 oz unsalted butter

3 Shape the mixture into 15 medium or 30 small burgers.

4 Beat the remaining eggs. Dip the burgers in beaten egg, and then lightly coat with flour.

5 Heat the oil in a frying-pan and shallow-fry the burgers until nicely browned and crisp on the outside.

to make the relish

1 Boil the corn on the cobs for 10–12 minutes. Remove from the pan and let cool slightly.

2 Slice off the corn kernels from the cob and put them in a pan. Add salt and pepper, red pepper, chillies, fresh marjoram and vegetable stock. Cook on a gentle heat until the liquid has reduced substantially.

3 Once the relish has reduced to a nice 'sloppy' consistency, melt the butter, whisk it up and stir it into the mixture. Check the seasoning.

to serve

1 Serve the burgers with the relish, salad and fries or as part of a seventies-revival, soul-food spread.

Miso Stir-fry

Getting into the Raw – Matt Fraser

serves six

1 tbspn vegetable oil

1 cm/½ in piece of fresh root ginger, peeled and cut into matchsticks)

bunch of spring onions, trimmed and chopped

1 fresh green chilli, seeded and chopped or sliced

medium-size head of broccoli, cut into florets

500 g/1 lb carrots, peeled and sliced

250 g/8 oz French beans, trimmed and cut in 2.5 cm/1 in lengths

2 large red peppers, seeded and cut in strips

2 tspn miso

2 tspn tahini

salt and pepper

1 Heat the oil in a wok or large, heavy-based frying-pan and sauté the ginger, spring onions and chilli for a minute.

2 Add the broccoli and carrots, with 1 tbspn of hot water and stir-fry for 2–3 minutes. Add the beans and peppers and continue cooking for a further 2–3 minutes.

3 Combine the miso and tahini with a little water, until smooth, and add to the pan. Continue cooking for a further minute or until the vegetables have softened a little but still retain their crunch. Season well with salt and pepper.

4 Serve immediately with pasta or rice.

Chestnut Kebabs

Christmas Tree – Tony Kitchell

serves six

900 g/2 lb sweet chestnuts
250 g/8 oz sun-dried tomatoes
2 aubergines, cut in 3 cm/1½ in chunks
2 red peppers, cut in 3 cm/1½ in squares
12 rosemary twigs, stripped and whittled to a point at one end

to pickle the chestnuts

2 sprigs of fresh tarragon
2 cloves of garlic
cider vinegar, enough to cover the chestnuts in a pan

for the marinade

120 g/4 oz fresh Parmesan, grated
900 ml/1½ pints red wine
150 ml/¼ pint olive oil
bunch of flat-leaf parsley, finely chopped
2 cloves of garlic, crushed

for the roasted tomato sauce

8 plum tomatoes
5 tbspn balsamic vinegar
4 tspn sugar
300 ml/½ pint water
few sprigs of fresh rosemary
salt and pepper

to pickle the chestnuts

1 Put the sweet chestnuts (still in their skins), tarragon and garlic in a pan and cover with the cider vinegar. Bring to the boil and then simmer for 15–20 minutes. Take off the heat and leave to soak in the vinegar for about a week.

2 After a week, peel the chestnuts, making sure that you get as much of the skin inside the shell off as possible.

to marinate the kebabs

1 Carefully thread the chestnuts, sun-dried tomatoes, aubergines and peppers on to the rosemary twigs.

2 Mix the parmesan, red wine, olive oil, parsley and garlic together in a large bowl and place the threaded kebabs in the mixture, to marinate for at least six hours.

to make the sauce

1 Preheat the oven to 180°C/350°F/Gas Mark 4. Cut the tomatoes into quarters and place in a shallow baking dish. Sprinkle with the balsamic vinegar and sugar and roast until the tomatoes have softened and caramelized.

2 Scrape all the tomatoes together and add the water and rosemary. Cook slowly for about 30 minutes.

3 When the tomatoes have completely dissolved, sieve the sauce to remove the skins and seeds. Add a little more water, if necessary. Season to taste with salt and pepper.

4 Roast the kebabs on the barbecue and serve with a little of the roasted tomato sauce.

Side Dishes

Italian-style Roast Potatoes

Yorkshire Sunday Best – Stewart Ibbotson

Fireman Stewart may think English roast beef is the greatest dish of all time but he follows tradition only up to a point. Instead of roasting potatoes in the fat around the joint, he now prefers to make Italian-style roast potatoes, cooked in olive oil and flavoured with basil, tomatoes and shallots.

serves five–six

150 ml/¼ pint olive oil

1 kg/2¼ lb new potatoes, washed and left whole

4 shallots, peeled and quartered

6 whole fresh basil leaves

3 fresh tomatoes, skinned, seeded and chopped

salt and freshly ground black pepper

1 Preheat the oven to 190°C/375°F/Gas mark 5.
2 In the oven, heat the oil in a baking dish or roasting tray.
3 Parboil the potatoes: put them in a pan of cold, well salted water and bring to the boil. Boil for just 1 minute, remove from the heat and drain.
4 Return the potatoes to the saucepan, cover with a lid and shake to slightly roughen the surface of the potatoes.
5 Add the potatoes and shallots to the oil and season with a little salt and pepper. Shake them around to coat with the oil and return to the oven.
6 After 30 minutes, add the basil, chopped tomatoes and seasoning.
7 Return to the oven for 15–20 minutes, until browned.
8 Serve with roast beef, or with any other meat or simply grilled fish.

Clare Montcrieff-Hunt's Fresh Mackerel in Plum Chutney Sauce

Lena Warboys' Three-Bird Roast

Pigeon Biter's Hare and Venison Pie

Nicky Samengo-Turner's Pasticcio

Niamh Watmore's Amaretti Chocolate Torte

Lorna Macleod's Damson Ice Cream with Sablées and Damson Sauce

Pigeon Biter's 'Boiled Baby'

Marion Postma's (Pozzi's) Pavlova

Rice and Peas

Caribbean Birthday Surprise – Trisha Wallace
and Alison Haughton

There are many variations on rice and peas in Caribbean cookery. This Jamaican version uses kidney beans instead of peas, which gives the dish a purply-pink colour and is particularly delicious with its flavourings of coconut and thyme.

serves six as a side dish

250 g/8 oz dried kidney beans, soaked overnight, drained and rinsed

375 g/12 oz long-grain rice (American or basmati)

1 onion, finely chopped

75 g/3 oz block of coconut cream, grated and dissolved in hot water

few sprigs of fresh thyme or ½ tspn dried thyme

1 Put the soaked beans in fresh water.
2 Bring to the boil and boil hard for 30 minutes to destroy the toxins in the beans.
3 Turn down the heat and cook until the beans are simmering and continue cooking until they are almost done. Drain, reserving the water.
4 Rinse the rice well. Put the rice, kidney beans and onion in a pan. Add the water in which the beans were cooked, topping it up if necessary, to get twice as much water by volume as rice and beans. Cook for about 10 minutes.
5 Add the coconut milk and thyme. Cook for another 10 minutes, or until all the liquid has been absorbed and the rice has cooked.
6 Serve on a big plate, surrounded by Fried Plantain (see page 133).

Yorkshire Pudding with Sage, Shallots and Sweet Onion Gravy

Yorkshire Sunday Best – Stewart Ibbotson

Yorkshire pudding is traditionally eaten in Yorkshire as a starter before the roast and served with gravy. The idea originally was to take the edge off the appetite, especially children's, so that nobody would be too hungry for the expensive meat that followed. Stewart has departed from tradition by adding sage and shallots to the batter, an idea picked up from his mother-in-law. The recipe for Sweet Onion Gravy was inspired by the chef Gary Rhodes, who is one of Stewart's culinary heroes for championing traditional British food. The onions are cooked gently for a very long time so they caramelize to a delicious savoury sweetness. Stewart says it is well worth the wait.

serves six–eight as a starter

250 g/8 oz plain flour

4 medium eggs

300 ml/½ pint milk

300 ml/½ pint water

4 small shallots, finely chopped

1½ tbspn finely chopped fresh sage or 1 tbspn dried sage

1½ tspn salt

freshly ground black pepper

75 g/3 oz lard, beef dripping or sunflower oil

1 Sift the flour into a large mixing basin and make a well in the middle. Add the eggs, one at a time, beating them into the flour with a fork. Bring in the flour gradually from the sides of the bowl and you should be able to avoid lumpiness.

2 Whisking constantly, slowly add enough milk and water to make a smooth batter the consistency of double cream.

3 Add the shallots and sage. Season with salt and pepper.

4 Leave covered with a tea-towel for at least 30 minutes and preferably for 1½ hours.

5 Preheat the oven to 230°C/450°F/Gas mark 8.

6 Put a large knob of lard, beef dripping or sunflower oil in two 20 cm/8 in round metal tins. Put in the oven until the fat starts to smoke (usually at least 15 minutes).

7 Pour the batter into the tins so that it covers the bottom but is no more than 1 cm/½ in deep.

8 Cook in the oven for 10–12 minutes, or until the puddings are puffed up, brown and crisp, turning round halfway through cooking.

for the gravy

2 tbspn sunflower oil,
lard or dripping

4 large onions, finely sliced

150 ml/5 fl oz water

850 ml/1½ pints beef stock

thickener if required

(1–2 tbspn of the Yorkshire
pudding batter or cornflour)

juices from the joint

a knob/15 g/½ oz butter

to make the gravy

1 Melt the fat in large saucepan or heavy frying pan over a medium heat and add the onions. Fry gently, stirring frequently to prevent sticking, until they are soft and well reduced in volume. Add a little water and go on cooking, stirring occasionally. The onions will slowly caramelize and turn sweet and golden. Whenever they seem in danger of getting too dry, or burning, add a little more of the water. You can go on cooking for up 2 hours, to get the softness, sweetness and caramel taste you want.

2 Add the stock. Turn up the heat and bubble to reduce for anything up to 30 minutes, until you have a sweet, beefy, oniony gravy. Thicken if you like by stirring in the Yorkshire pudding batter or a little cornflour.

3 Add the meat juices from the roasting joint and a knob of butter to glaze.

4 Serve half with the Yorkshire pudding and save the rest to serve with the roast beef.

Refried Beans

The Chilli Boys – Eddie Baines and Steve Donovan

serves six

175 g/6 oz black kidney beans
or pinto beans, soaked
overnight, drained and rinsed

1–2 tbspn vegetable oil

75 g/3 oz mature Cheddar or
manchego cheese, grated

salt and freshly ground
black pepper

1 Put the beans in plenty of fresh water and bring to the boil, cooking at a full rolling boil for at least 45 minutes or until tender (with dried beans that have been hanging around for a long time this can take up to 2 hours). It does not matter if the beans are over-cooked because they are going to be mashed up. Drain.

2 Put the cooked beans in 1 tbspn oil and cook over a medium heat, mashing every so often with a potato masher so they absorb the oil. Add a little more oil if the beans get too dry. Continue until you get a dryish, thick, heavy bean paste.

3 Mash in the cheese and season with salt and pepper. Cook for another minute, mixing thoroughly, and check the seasoning.

4 Refried beans are used in all kinds of Mexican dishes, but a satisfyingly simple way to serve them is to fill a taco shell or soft tortilla, add extra cheese, melt in a hot oven for a few minutes and serve with red chilli sauce at one end, soured cream at the other, and lots of guacamole in the middle. Accompany with soft tortillas (see page 110) or include as part of a Mexican feast.

Parsnip Purée

Colin and Duncan's Black Tie Dinner – Colin Beattie

This creamy mash is delicious with roast meats and game.

serves four

500 g/1 lb parsnips

250 g/8 oz potatoes, peeled

2 cloves of garlic

175 ml/6 fl oz milk

175 g/6 oz butter

½ tspn wholegrain mustard

pinch of grated nutmeg

salt and pepper

1 Cook the potatoes and parsnips in the same pan, until just tender.

2 Cool the parsnips and then top, tail and skin them.

3 Process both vegetables with a hand-held blender until smooth (*do not use a food processor or you will end up with glue!*).

4 Warm the milk with the garlic and leave to infuse. Discard the garlic.

5 Add the butter, milk and seasoning to the parsnip purée and re-heat gently. Or let it cool and re-heat later.

Fried Plantains

Caribbean Birthday Surprise – Tricia Wallace and Alison Haughton

Plantains are a large, starchy member of the banana family. When buying a plantain, make sure that the skin is black and it is tender when gently pressed (an unripe plantain can still have a black skin), but not too soft or bruised by squeezing. If not quite ready to eat, plantains can be left to ripen on a window-sill.

serves eight

2–3 plantains

salt

1 tspn caster sugar

sunflower or other vegetable oil, for frying

1 Peel and slice the plantain in 6 mm/¼ in thick slices, cut crossways at an angle. Sprinkle a little salt and sugar over each piece.

2 Heat 5 cm/2 in oil in a deep pan so it is hot enough for deep-frying (i.e. a little piece of bread will sizzle and start to brown after about 20 seconds).

3 Fry the plantain slices in batches for 2 or 3 minutes, turning over once, until browned.

4 Drain on kitchen paper and sprinkle with more salt, if wanted.

Gratin Dauphinois

Late Starter – Wendy Ingham

serves six as a side dish

2 cloves of garlic

150 g/5 oz butter

salt and white pepper

1.25 kg/3 lb floury potatoes,
peeled, washed and thinly sliced

750 ml/1¼ pints double cream
(or, for a lighter dish, half milk
and half cream)

1 Preheat the oven to 200°C/400°F/Gas mark 6.

2 Rub an ovenproof dish all over with a garlic clove, and then butter generously with half the butter.

3 Season the potatoes well with salt and pepper – be generous as they need plenty of seasoning. Layer the potatoes in the dish.

4 Bring the cream to the boil with the remaining garlic clove; then pour over the potatoes, removing the garlic clove.

5 Dot the surface of the gratin with the remaining butter.

6 Put in the oven and bake for 10 minutes. Then reduce the oven to 150°C/300°F/Gas mark 2 for a further 20–30 minutes. The surface should be brown and the potatoes creamy.

7 The gratin is now ready to serve, but it can be left to cool, refrigerated and kept for up to two days. Individual servings can be stamped out with a pastry cutter, wrapped in foil to keep their shape (but leave the top open) and reheated for 15 minutes in a hot (190°C/375°F/Gas mark 5) oven.

Note: If making a lighter dish with half milk and half cream, boil the milk and cream separately, to prevent curdling. Pour them separately over the potatoes.

Bhurta (Aubergine Masala)

The Korachi Club – Nina and Sumita Dhand

serves eight

6 large aubergines

butter

3–4 tbspn vegetable oil

1 tspn ground jeera (cumin)

1 large onion, finely chopped

1 tspn haldi (ground tumeric)

fresh red chilli, seeded

2 tomatoes, finely chopped

salt

3 tbspn chopped fresh coriander

2 fresh green chillies, seeded
and finely chopped

garam masala (optional)

1 Grease the aubergines with butter and then roast them over the gas flame or under the grill. When the aubergine is completely blackened take off the heat and leave to cool.

2 Heat the oil in a pan. Add the jeera and brown. Then add the onions and sauté. Add the haldi and red chilli. Allow to cook for a few minutes.

3 When the aubergines are cool enough to handle, peel off the skin and chop the flesh.

4 Add the tomatoes and cook through. Add the chopped aubergines and a little bit of salt. "Bhunna" for 10 minutes, that is, beat hard with a wooden spoon until the oil begins to separate and you achieve a nice rich consistency.

5 Before serving, add some chopped coriander and finely chopped green chillies. Garam masala can be added at the end, if wanted.

Irish Whiskey Tarka Dhal

Five Nations Rugby Curry – Gerry Mansfield

Sloshing whisky into Tarka Dhal sounds like a rash act, but it works surprisingly well.

serves a rugby team! (fifteen)

750 g/1½ lb red or mansoor lentils

4 tbspn ghee

4 large onions, 2 finely chopped, 2 thinly sliced

4 tspn ginger purée

10 cloves of garlic, chopped

2 tspn ground turmeric

8 dried chillies

2.5 litres/4 pints vegetable stock

2 tspn garam masala

salt

4 tbspn Jameson's Irish Whiskey

1 Thoroughly wash and pick over the lentils.

2 Melt half the ghee in a large pan and fry the finely chopped onions, ginger and garlic until the onion is light brown.

3 Stir in the turmeric and then add the lentils and chillies and fry for 2 minutes. Add the stock, bring to the boil, skim off any scum from the surface, then simmer for 35–40 minutes, stirring occasionally.

4 Meanwhile, heat the remaining ghee and fry the sliced onions until dark brown and almost burnt. Remove from the heat and reserve.

5 When the lentils have reached the consistency of porridge, stir in the browned onions and garam masala. Season with salt. Cook for a further 2 minutes before serving. Pour the whiskey over the lentils at the table and mix in well.

6 Serve with Gerry's other dishes – see **The Cooks** section on page 178.

Wynne's Super Creamy Mashed Potatoes

Wynne's Last Supper – Wynne Fearfield

After experimenting with dozens of ways of making mash, Wynne has settled on the painstaking method of pushing the potatoes through a sieve with a wooden spoon to get a fine, silky-smooth purée. A mouli-légumes also works for this purée but never use a food processor, as it will break down the starch and make the potatoes gluey. Wynne uses unsalted butter and, occasionally, olive oil or butter mixed with an egg yolk for added richness but shuns milk, which, she says, produces a less good taste and a runny texture. Wynne's top spud for mash is Desirée, followed by (in no particular order) Romano, Cara, Estima, King Edwards, Marsona, Elvira, Pentland Squire, Maris Piper or Bintje.

serves six

900 g/2 lb Desirée potatoes, peeled and cut into quarters

120 g/4 oz unsalted butter

salt and freshly ground black pepper

1 Put the potatoes in a pan of salted cold water. Bring to the boil and simmer until tender. Do not boil too hard as this often makes the potatoes disintegrate or leaves the centre hard when the outside is cooked.

2 Drain the potatoes in a colander and let them dry for a couple of minutes.

3 Purée the potatoes through a sieve or mouli-légumes into a clean saucepan. Add the butter. Heat gently so the butter melts and can be stirred into the potato. Season with salt and pepper.

Brussel Sprouts Pan-fried with Pancetta

Colin and Duncan's Black Tie Dinner – Colin Beattie

serves eight

120 g/4 oz butter

275 g/9 oz pancetta, cubed

900 g/2 lb brussels sprouts, trimmed and shredded

salt and pepper

1 Melt the butter in a frying-pan and add the pancetta.

2 Fry until golden brown and the fat is going crisp.

3 Add the sprouts to the fried pancetta and pan-fry until the sprouts are just wilting.

4 Season and serve with Colin and Duncan's Stuffed Quail with Gooseberry Marmalade (see **The Cooks** section) or other poultry and game dishes.

Bombay 'Tatties & Neeps'

Five Nations Rugby Curry – Gerry Mansfield

For obvious reasons, this dish represented Scotland in Gerry's 'Five Nations' curry spread. I don't suppose swedes are even known in India, but they respond very well to curry spices.

serves a rugby team! (fifteen)

1.25 kg/3 lb potatoes,
peeled and diced

900 g/2 lb swede,
peeled and diced

5 tbspn ghee or cooking oil

2 tbspn black mustard seeds

2 tspn ground turmeric

3 large onions,
thinly sliced into rings

4 tspn chilli powder

1 tspn ground cumin

1 tspn salt

1 Boil the potatoes and swede together for 10 minutes. Drain and keep warm.

2 Heat the ghee or oil in a large pan and add the mustard seeds. As the mustard seeds begin to pop, add the turmeric and fry for 30 seconds. Add the onions, mix thoroughly and fry until soft.

3 Add the potatoes and swede and mix well. Add the chilli, cumin and salt and fry until cooked (about 5 minutes). Serve with Gerry's other Indian recipes listed in **The Cooks** section on page 178.

Desserts

Cakes and Tarts

Pat's Coconut Pie

*Caribbean Birthday Surprise – Trisha Wallace
and Alison Haughton*

An authentic Caribbean recipe from Alison's mother, Pat, which was
served as one of the birthday cakes at Trisha's flatmate, Amaka's
surprise birthday dinner.

Serves eight to ten

for the pastry

250 g/8 oz plain flour
1 tbspn caster sugar
1 tbspn ground almonds
120 g/4 oz butter
a little cold water

To make the pastry

1 Preheat the oven to 200°C/400°F/Gas mark 6.

2 Sift the flour into a bowl. Mix with the sugar and
ground almonds.

3 Cut the butter into small pieces. Mix with the
flour to get a breadcrumb texture. Add a little
cold water and mix together to form a ball. Rest
in the fridge for 15 minutes.

4 Roll out the pastry and put into a 23 cm/9 in
pastry case. Trim the edges, prick the base and
refrigerate.

5 *Optional:* if you want the pastry crisp, you can
bake the pastry case blind. Line with foil and
pour in dried beans or clay baking beads. Bake
for 15 minutes at 180°C/350°F/Gas mark 4.
Remove the foil and beans, and return to the
oven for 2 more minutes to dry out the pastry
case. Remove and either add the filling straight
away or set the pastry case aside until you are
ready for it. (Then turn up the oven to
200°C/400°F/Gas mark 6 again for the tart.)

▶

for the filling

300 ml/½ pint hot milk, or
½ milk and ½ double cream for
a slightly richer pie

50 g/2 oz caster sugar

pinch of salt

pinch of grated nutmeg

120 g/4 oz fresh coconut flesh,
grated

1 tspn vanilla essence

3 egg yolks, beaten

for the topping

3 egg whites

120 g/4 oz caster sugar

½ tspn vanilla essence

pinch of cream of tartar

10 glacé cherries, to decorate

To make the filling

1 Mix together the hot milk, caster sugar, salt, nutmeg, coconut and vanilla essence. Slowly add the egg yolks, mixing well.

2 Pour into the pastry case (blind or otherwise) and bake in the oven for 10 minutes.

3 Reduce the oven heat to 170°C/325°F/Gas mark 3 and continue baking the pie for a further 35 minutes, or until the filling has set. Remove from the oven and allow to cool.

4 Turn the oven back up to 200°C/400°F/Gas mark 6.

To make the topping

1 Whisk the egg whites until they hold peaks.

2 Slowly add the caster sugar, vanilla essence and cream of tartar, whisking as you go. Continue to beat until stiff.

3 Spread the meringue over the top of the filling, right to the edges.

4 Decorate with glacé cherries. Bake for 10 minutes, or until the top is bronzed.

5 Serve hot or cold.

Chocolate and Coffee Mousse Cakes

Late Starter – Wendy Ingham

The joy of this indulgent dessert is that it is rich with chocolate and cream but still has a light texture.

serves six

for the sponge

2 eggs, separated

50 g/2 oz caster sugar

50 g/2 oz plain flour

40 g/1½ oz butter, melted and left to cool

for the mousse

150 g/5 oz good-quality chocolate (at least 55 per cent cocoa solids)

1 tspn strong coffee granules

2 egg yolks

1 tspn Cointreau (optional)

500 ml/18 fl oz double cream, whipped fairly stiffly

10 ml/½ fl oz water

2 tbspn granulated sugar

2 tbspn dark rum

grated chocolate (optional decoration)

finely shredded orange zest (optional decoration)

chocolate-covered coffee beans (optional decoration)

to make the sponge

1 Preheat the oven to 170°C/325°F/Gas mark 3.

2 Beat the egg whites until the whisk leaves soft peaks, then add the sugar while beating continually.

3 Whisk in the egg yolks, then carefully fold in the flour.

4 Add the butter and stir gently.

5 Pour the mixture on to a baking sheet lined with greaseproof paper. Spread to approximately 1.5 cm/½ in thick.

6 Cook for 10 minutes, then leave to cool on a wire rack.

to make the mousse

1 Break the chocolate into small pieces and place with the coffee in a double-boiler or a bowl over a pan of simmering water and melt. Do not allow the water to boil for more than a few seconds before taking it off the heat. Stir the chocolate until it is smooth.

2 Remove from the heat and stir in the egg yolks with a wooden spoon and the Cointreau if using.

3 Stir one-third of the whipped cream into the melted chocolate and then gently fold the chocolate into the rest of the cream.

▶

4 Make a syrup by placing 10 ml/½ fl oz of water into a saucepan and add 2 tbspn sugar. Bring to the boil and simmer until all the sugar has dissolved and the liquid has reduced by half. Add the rum and leave to cool.

5 Place an 8 cm/3 in baking ring over the sponge base and cut a disc. Transfer the disc and ring to a serving plate. Repeat for the five other servings.

6 Brush the sponge disc inside the ring with the syrup, then fill the ring with the mousse mixture, making sure to leave no gaps. Repeat for all the servings. Refrigerate, with the baking rings, until required.

7 Carefully remove the rings and decorate as desired. Suggestions: sprinkle the plate with finely grated dark chocolate and shreds of orange zest, or serve with chocolate-covered coffee beans.

Sweet Potato Pudding

A Jamaican Farewell – Paige Mulroy

serves eight

250 ml/8 fl oz double cream

1 tspn grated nutmeg

1 tspn ground cinnamon

250 ml/8 fl oz coconut milk

120 g/4 oz brown sugar

6 eggs, beaten

75 g/3 oz raisins

1 tspn vanilla essence

1 large sweet potato, peeled and grated

1 Preheat the oven to 150°C/300°F/Gas mark 3. Combine all the ingredients except the sweet potato and purée until smooth.

2 Add to the sweet potato and mix together.

3 Pour into a buttered baking dish and bake in a slow oven for one hour.

4 Serve with 'Irish Mist' or Bailey's Irish Cream liqueur poured over, as a sauce.

Prune and Armagnac Tart

The French Connection – Selina Snow

Artist Selina Snow took her father (and me) on a day trip to Boulogne to buy ther ingredients for his birthday supper. Idriss, at 16 Grande Rue, was perhaps Selina's favourite shop in Boulogne, selling nothing but dried fruit and nuts of supreme quality and dazzling appearance. The Agen prunes she bought were the plumpest, juiciest and most flavourful I have ever encountered, transforming this tart from something special into something sensational. Vary the recipe with the season. Cherries soaked in Marsala are good in the summer, for example.

Serves four–eight, depending on greed!

approximately 15 plump prunes (ideally from Agen)

120 ml/4 fl oz/a generous wine glass of Armagnac

for the pastry case

250 g/8 oz plain flour (preferably organic)

2 tbspn caster sugar

120 g/4 oz unsalted butter, chilled

1 free-range egg

for the custard filling

200 ml/7 fl oz crème fraîche

75 g/3 oz caster sugar

3 free-range eggs

few drops of vanilla essence (or use sugar that has had a vanilla pod stored in it)

1 Soak the prunes in Armagnac for at least an hour, or overnight if they are very dry. Remove any stones.

to make the pastry case

1 Preheat the oven to 190°C/375°F/Gas mark 5. Blend together the flour, sugar and butter in a food processor or by hand, until the mixture resembles breadcrumbs.

2 With the motor running, add the egg to bind the mixture together. Chill the pastry for at least half an hour.

3 Roll out the pastry on a floured surface and line a 23 cm/9 in baking tin. Put in the fridge or freezer for 15 minutes, then line the pastry case with foil and fill with baking beans. Bake for 20 minutes and then remove the foil and beans carefully and bake for another 2 minutes.

▶

to make the filling

1 Blend the crème fraîche, sugar, eggs and vanilla essence together in a food processor or by hand with a balloon whisk.

2 Drain the prunes and put in the bottom of the cooked pastry case, then pour over the custard mixture.

3 Bake for 30–40 minutes, until firm and golden. Serve warm or at room temperature.

Amaretti Chocolate Torte

Scouts Honour – Niamh Watmore

This was the triumphant finale to Niamh's surprise Scout's feast. It's a dreamy dish for chocoholics young and old.

serves eight

groundnut oil, for brushing

100 g/3½ oz Amaretti biscuits, crushed

500 g/1 lb plain dark chocolate

5 tbspn liquid glucose

3 tbspn rum

600 ml/1 pint double cream

groundnut oil

1 Line the base of a 23 cm/9 in cake tin with baking parchment and brush the sides with groundnut oil.

2 Sprinkle the crushed biscuits over the base of the tin.

3 Put the chocolate, liquid glucose and rum in a bowl over a pan of barely simmering water. Do not stir until the chocolate has melted.

4 Take off the heat and stir quickly. Leave for 5 minutes.

5 Whip the cream until slightly thickened.

6 Fold half the cream into the chocolate mixture; beat together.

7 Then fold the chocolate mixture into the other half of the cream. Pour into the tin.

8 Tap the tin to remove any air pockets. Cover with cling film and chill in the fridge for at least 3 hours or overnight.

Baked Tofu Cheesecake

Getting into the Raw – Matt Fraser

I was highly sceptical about Matt Fraser's claim that his vegan cheesecake would taste as good as any dairy version of the dish. But in the end I had to eat my words, along with a second slice of cheesecake.

serves six–eight

for the biscuit base

120 g/4 oz soya or vegetable margarine, melted

300 g/10 oz digestive biscuits, finely crushed

for the topping

300 ml/½ pint milk (preferably soya milk)

2 x 250 g/8 oz packets of plain tofu

8 tbspn vegetable oil

1 tspn vanilla essence

4 tbspn orange-flower water

2 tbspn maple syrup

1 tbspn pumpkin seeds

1 Preheat the oven to 180°C/350°F/Gas mark 4. Melt the margarine in a saucepan and add the crushed digestive biscuits. Press over the base of a 20 cm/8 in loose-bottomed flan tin or ovenproof dish. Place in the fridge for 10 minutes, to harden.

2 Purée the soya milk, tofu, oil, vanilla essence and orange-flower water, until smooth. (You may have to do this in batches.)

3 Pour the filling into the chilled base. Drizzle the maple syrup over the top of the pudding and sprinkle with pumpkin seeds. Bake for 30–40 minutes.

4 Remove from the oven and chill for at least 2 hours. Serve cold, cut into wedges.

Pecan Pie

Leaving Liverpool – Jon Ashton

Jon Ashton is a cheeky Scouser with a penchant for adding his own imaginative twist to classic dishes (see his recipe for Black Pudding Wontons with Balsamic Sauce). Here Southern Comfort was the extra ingredient, and it's not just a gratuitous slosh of booze. The zesty orange overtures of the spirit work very well with the maple and pecan.

serves four

for the pastry

250 g/8 oz plain flour

¼ tspn baking powder

½ tspn ground cinnamon

¼ tspn grated nutmeg

pinch of ground cloves

pinch of salt

3 tbspn sugar

50 g/2 oz cold salted butter

1 egg

for the filling

500 g/1 lb pecan nuts

120 ml/4 fl oz maple syrup

120 ml/4 fl oz golden syrup

175 g/6 oz sugar

75 g/3 oz butter

3 large eggs, whisked

scant 1 tbspn Southern Comfort

1 Preheat the oven to 200°C/400°F/Gas mark 6.

2 To make the pastry, sift the dry ingredients together and stir in the sugar. Rub in the butter until the mixture resembles fine breadcrumbs. Add the egg and mix to a dough. Wrap the dough in foil or cling film and leave to rest in the fridge for 1 hour.

3 Roll out the pastry and line a 20 cm/8 in pie tin.

4 Lightly press the pecan nuts into the pastry.

5 Heat both syrups in a pan, add the sugar and stir until dissolved. Add the butter, whisked eggs and Southern Comfort and stir until well mixed.

6 Pour the mixture into the pie case and bake for 40 minutes, until golden brown. Serve with cream.

American Devil's Food Cake

Dinner with the Dawsons – Peggy Dawson

serves six to eight

for the cake

300 g/10 oz plain flour
400 g/14 oz caster sugar
175 g/6 oz cocoa powder
1 tspn bicarbonate of soda
½ tspn baking powder
1 tspn salt
175 g/6 oz margarine
1 tspn vanilla essence
300 ml/½ pint milk
3 eggs

for the filling

1–2 tbspn cassis
250 ml/8 fl oz double cream
sugar, to taste
200 g/7 oz blackcurrants, stewed

for the icing

250 ml/½ pint double cream
250 g/8 oz couverture or good-quality plain chocolate (at least 45% cocoa solids)

to decorate

edible flowerheads
1 egg white, lightly beaten
caster sugar

to make the cake

1 Preheat the oven to 190°C/375°F/Gas mark 5. Beat together the flour, caster sugar, cocoa powder, bicarbonate of soda, baking powder, salt, margarine, vanilla essence and 180ml/ 6 fl oz of the milk. Beat together for about 2½ minutes. Add the rest of the milk and the eggs and beat for a further 2½ minutes.

2 Put into two greased 23 cm/9 in tins and bake for 40 minutes. Allow to cool.

to make the filling

1 Sprinkle both cakes with cassis.

2 Beat the double cream with some sugar until thick. Spread on the bottom layer of the cake. Add a layer of the stewed blackcurrants. Sandwich the two cakes together.

to make the icing

1 Bring the double cream to the boil and slowly add the *couverture*. Allow to cool and then spread over the top and sides of the cake.

to decorate

1 To make frosted flowers to decorate, dip perfect edible flowerheads in egg white and then in caster sugar and leave to dry.

Mousses, Ices and Fruit Desserts

Mango Fool

Gordon's Table – Gordon Perrier

Gordon says the Alfonsa mangoes which come into season in India in May are the best mangoes in the world. He has enjoyed gluts of mangoes when visiting family and friends in India. 'In India, you would eat them simply in the bathtub with a fan blowing a cool breeze from the veranda and the faint sound of hawkers busying themselves on the street outside,' he says. This pudding is another way of enjoying this magnificent fruit, any time of the year.

serves two

4 large, ripe mangoes

2 tbspn thick double cream

75 g/3 oz caster sugar

¼ bulb stem ginger, roughly chopped

1 Preheat the oven to 180°C/350°F/Gas mark 4.
2 Cut two mangoes in half and tease out the stones. Take the centre flesh out of each half, leaving a thin layer on the skin. Get as much flesh as possible from the other two mangoes. Cut all the mango flesh into rough cubes.
3 Put the chopped mango in a baking dish, cover with foil and cook in the oven for 25–30 minutes. Remove and leave to cool.
4 When cool, whiz the fruit to a purée in a food processor, with the cream, sugar and ginger.
5 Spoon the mixture into the scooped-out skin of the four mango halves. Freeze for half an hour before serving. Put two halves back together to present each mango as a whole fruit.

Chocolate Orange Pots

A Vegan Theatre Picnic – Rachel Markham

serves four

175 g/6 oz 'Green & Blacks' organic plain chocolate

1 packet of soft, silken tofu

grated zest and juice of 1 orange

2–3 tbspn rum

2–3 tbspn Cointreau

extra melted chocolate and edible violets, to decorate

1 Melt the chocolate gently and carefully.

2 Purée the tofu until smooth.

3 Add the melted chocolate to the tofu and mix together well.

4 Add the orange zest and juice and a generous splash each of rum and Cointreau. Purée everything until smooth.

5 Pour into a jug and, working quickly, before the mixture sets, pour into glasses. Allow to set fully in the fridge, for at least 3 hours or overnight.

6 Decorate the tops with chocolate piping and edible violets.

Sweet White Wine Granita with Mixed Berries

Tuscany-by-Doncaster – Michael Masserella

This refreshing ice is really easy to make, using any sweet or dessert wine and any berries. The advantage of a granita over a sorbet is that you don't have to interrupt the freezing process with endless whisking – the mixture is allowed to freeze solid, then texture is created by scraping it into crystals with a fork.

serves four–six

375 ml/12 fl oz sweet white wine

45 g/1½ oz granulated sugar

120 ml/4 fl oz water

250 g/8 oz mixed summer berries, e.g. strawberries, raspberries, redcurrants, and/or blackberries

juice of ½ lemon

2 cinnamon sticks

150 ml/¼ pint whipping cream, softly whipped (optional)

1 Boil the wine, sugar and water, stirring occasionally, until the sugar has dissolved and you have a syrupy consistency.

2 Set aside a few of the best berries for decoration. In a mixing bowl, with a wooden spoon (not metal), crush the rest of the berries so that they release their juices. Add these to the pan, with the lemon juice and cinnamon sticks, and simmer for several more minutes.

3 Strain the mixture through a fine sieve into a shallow glass baking dish or plastic dish. Cover with cling film and put in the freezer for 3–4 hours, or overnight, until frozen solid.

4 Chill a deep serving glass for each person in the freezer for a couple of hours. When you take them out, the glasses will have a frosted appearance.

5 Just before you want to eat, fork the surface granita into soft, snowy crystals.

6 Place some berries in each glass. Top with granita and then the whipped cream, if you are using it. Add more berries and serve at once, with frittelle or biscotti.

Italian Breasts in Sunshine

A Futurist Feast – Celia Lyttleton

A very simple and delicious dessert is created by simply mixing very fresh ricotta cheese with sliced fresh strawberries. I wouldn't hesitate to serve the mixture at a dinner party, though not necessarily in the same way as Celia did at her Futurist Feast. She was determined to introduce an erotic note into the proceedings by insisting that guests tackled the breast-shaped mounds without cutlery and with their hands tied behind their backs.

serves eight to ten

1 kg/2¼ lb very fresh ricotta cheese

500 g/1 lb strawberries, washed, hulled and quartered

1 capful Crème de Cassis

2 raspberries

runny honey

pink or red rose petals, to decorate

1 Put the ricotta, strawberries and cassis in a large mixing bowl and mix together very gently, so the cheese retains its fairly stiff texture.

2 Divide the mixture into two equal mounds on a large serving plate and, using a spatula or wide knife, mould them into smooth mounds – 'as high and proud as you can make them,' according to Celia.

3 When you are satisfied with your breasts, take the two raspberries, dip them in honey and put one on top of each mound.

4 Just before serving, scatter fresh rose petals all around the breasts.

Gin and Tonic Sorbet

The Policeman's Ball – Paul Francey

This recipe was made to serve 60, as an inter-course palate-cleanser at Paul Francey's riotous Policeman's Ball. You may want to reduce the quantities somewhat!

serves sixty

750 g/1½ lb caster sugar

1.75 litres/3 pints water

grated zest and juice of 6 lemons

¾ bottle gin

1.5 litres/2½ pints tonic water

24 egg whites

1 Make a sugar syrup by dissolving the sugar in the water on the stove. Boil until the temperature reaches soft-ball stage (120°C/250°F).

2 When the syrup reaches the correct temperature, add the lemon zest and juice. Add the gin and tonic and mix thoroughly. (More gin or tonic can be added for taste.)

3 Pour the mixture into a plastic container and, when cool, freeze for a couple of hours, until it becomes a thick sludge.

4 Beat 24 egg whites until stiff. When the gin and tonic mixture has frozen to a sludge, gently combine it with the beaten egg white and when thoroughly mixed, return to the plastic container and freeze.

5 Remove from the freezer about 30 minutes before serving.

Calvados Sorbet

Gourmet Night – Gordon Irvine

Gordon likes to serve this as a pudding or between courses to clean the palate so that the flavours in the next course taste strong and fresh. Calvados is also a good digestif.

serves six

175 g/6 oz caster sugar

450 ml/¾ pint water

thinly pared zest and juice of a large lemon

50 ml/2 fl oz Calvados

1 egg white

1 Heat the sugar and water in a saucepan over a low heat, stirring with a wooden spoon, until all the sugar has dissolved. Turn up the heat, bring to the boil and bubble rapidly for 5 minutes to get a light syrup.

2 Take the pan off the heat, add the lemon zest and juice, and leave to cool.

3 Pour the sugar syrup and Calvados into an ice-cream maker. While this is on, whisk the egg white until it is standing in soft peaks.

4 When the syrup is beginning to set in the ice-cream maker, fold in the egg white and return to the ice-cream machine for another 2–3 minutes. Pour into a container and put in the freezer. If making this by hand, put the mixture into a plastic container and freeze until it starts to set (30 minutes to an hour). Whisk the frozen edges back into the syrup and return to the freezer. Repeat the exercise and you should have a nicely slushy half-frozen mixture. Fold in the whisked egg white thoroughly and return the mixture to the freezer until completely hard.

5 If the sorbet is very hard, take it out of the freezer about 45 minutes before serving. You may not need to do this because the alcohol stops it from freezing too hard.

Damson Ice Cream with Sablées and Damson Sauce

A Literary Dinner – Lorna Macleod

(Pâte sablée based on a recipe from The Roux Brothers on Pâtisserie, *Little, Brown & Co., 1993).*

serves twelve

for the pâte Sablée

200 g/7 oz butter, softened

100 g/3½ oz icing sugar, sifted

pinch of salt

2 egg yolks

drop of bitter almond essence

250 g/8 oz flour, sifted

for the damson purée

1 kg/2¼ lb damsons

150 ml/¼ pint sugar syrup

for the damson sauce

juice from cooking damsons

icing sugar, to taste

Armagnac and Amaretto, to taste

to make the pâte sablée

1 Put the softened butter into a food processor, with the icing sugar, salt and egg yolks. Mix well. Add a drop of bitter almond essence and then add the sifted flour and mix, just until it forms a dough. Do not over-process. Roll into a ball and chill for a couple of hours.

2 Preheat the oven to 200°C/400°F/Gas mark 6. Roll the pastry out and, using a pastry cutter, cut into twenty-four rounds, the same size as the rings in which the ice cream will be made. Put on lightly greased baking sheets.

3 Bake the *sablées* for about 10 minutes, until golden brown.

to make the damson purée

1 Wash and drain the damsons. Put into a stainless-steel saucepan and add just enough water to cover. Bring to the boil and simmer gently until the damsons are tender.

2 Strain the fruit and put the juice back in the pan. Reduce over a low heat to about one-third of its original volume.

3 Meanwhile, sieve the cooked fruit. Add some sugar syrup to the resulting purée. Do not add too much – just enough to take away the acidity but not enough to make it very sweet.

▶

for the ice cream base

75 g/3 oz caster sugar

190 ml/6.6 fl oz water

3 egg yolks

450 ml/¾ pint double cream

to decorate

fresh redcurrants

1 egg white, lightly beaten

caster sugar

icing sugar, sifted

to make the damson sauce

1 While the juice is still warm, add some icing sugar to taste. The sauce should not be too sweet. Then add the Armagnac and Amaretto to taste. The sauce should be syrupy but not too thick in texture.

to make the ice cream base

1 Put the sugar and water in a small pan and dissolve over a low heat. Beat the egg yolks until they become pale in colour and slightly thickened. In another pan, scald the cream and allow to cool. Once the sugar is completely dissolved, bring to the boil and cook rapidly to 220°C/425°F. Allow to cool. Slowly whisk the egg yolks in the food processor as the sugar syrup is poured in, in a steady stream. Continue whisking until thick and mousse-like. Cool thoroughly, then add the cream.

2 Set twelve 10 cm/4 in deep stainless-steel rings on a baking tray lined with baking parchment. Make sure that it will fit in the freezer. Chill the equipment in the freezer while you combine the damson purée with the mousse. Check the sweetness and add more sugar syrup if necessary. Churn the mixture in the ice-cream maker according to the manufacturer's instructions.

3 Carefully fill the rings with ice cream, pressing down well. Finish off the surface with a spatula. Place in the freezer.

to make the sugared redcurrants

1 Dip small bunches of redcurrants in the egg white and then in caster sugar and leave to dry.

▶

to serve

1 If the ice cream has been in the freezer overnight, take it out and put it into the fridge to soften for half an hour before serving. If made on the same day, it can come straight out of the freezer.

2 Dust half the *sablées* with icing sugar. Pour a small amount of the damson sauce on to each plate and carefully spread it out. Run a thin knife around the ice cream and gently push out from the rings – place each ice cream on the unsugared *sablées*. Place the sugared *sablées* on top. Place the ice creams in the centre of the plates.

3 Decorate with the sugared redcurrants.

Rambutan Ice Cream

Rumble in the Jungle – Felicity Keebaugh

This ice uses tinned rambutans but Felicity likes to decorate it with fresh rambutans – if she can find them – because she thinks they look like little hairy monsters!

serves six

2 x 400 g/14 oz tins of rambutans

juice of 1 lime

approximately 2 tbspn sugar, to taste

3 eggs, separated

12 fresh rambutans, to decorate (optional)

1 Drain the rambutans. Put in the food processor or liquidizer and process to a pulp.

2 Transfer to a mixing bowl and add the lime juice and sugar.

3 Beat the whites until stiff and fold into the rambutan purée.

4 Put the mixture in a plastic dish and freeze.

5 Put the frozen mixture in a food processor and beat up until it is slushy.

6 Add two of the egg yolks and beat until smooth. Return to the freezer and leave until solid.

7 Remove about 30 minutes before serving, to soften slightly. Pile spoonfuls of the ice into glasses. Decorate with half-peeled fresh rambutans if you can find them.

Passion-fruit Mousse in Filo Baskets with a Raspberry Coulis and Cape Gooseberries

Gourmet Night – Gordon Irvine

This pudding, which is the creation of Gordon's wife, Liz, gives a fresh, fruity lift to the end of a meal when your appetite has started to weary. Gordon finds leaf gelatine easier to use than the powdered variety. He discovered some French passion-fruit purée in his wholesale suppliers in Glasgow: it is certainly a useful short cut to scooping out a lot of passion fruits by hand. Filo pastry can be bought frozen in most good supermarkets. It is delicate stuff, but easy enough to deal with if you handle it according to the instructions on the packet. Most of all, keep it covered and do not let it dry out.

serves six

for the filo-pastry baskets

6 sheets filo pastry

45 g/1½ oz butter, melted

1 Preheat the oven to 180°C/350°F/Gas mark 4.

2 Brush the pastry sheets with butter. Fold in four, buttering the pastry each time you fold it. Butter six heat-proof cup moulds or small ramekins, roughly 5 x 2 cm/2 x 1 in. They should be flat-bottomed if possible, such as dariole moulds.

3 Place in the preheated oven until golden brown (about 5 minutes). Keep checking on the baskets after 3 minutes as they burn easily. Make the baskets in batches if you have only two or three suitable moulds.

4 Remove from the oven and carefully take the baskets off their moulds. Put back in the oven until crisp, right-way up if the moulds are flat-bottomed or on their sides if they are rounded. Remove from the oven and leave to cool on a wire rack.

▶

for the mousse

2 x 3 g (⅛ fl oz) sheets
gelatine leaf

175 g/6 oz passion-fruit
purée or the pulp of
15–20 passion fruit

approximately 1–2 tbspn icing
sugar, to taste

175 ml/6 fl oz double cream

75 ml/3 fl oz crème fraîche

1 Cover the gelatine in cold water to soften.

2 Put the passion-fruit purée into a bowl. Add icing sugar a little at a time, to taste. You can add little or none if you like it very tart.

3 Whip the double cream until stiff. Fold the crème fraîche into the whipped cream.

4 Fold the cream mixture into the passion-fruit purée. Taste and add more icing sugar if desired.

5 Pour off water from gelatine leaves and melt the leaf in the microwave (full power for 30–40 seconds) or heat the soaked gelatine gently in a little water until it has dissolved.

6 Pour the melted gelatine into the mousse mixture, folding it in very briskly.

7 Pour the mixture into the filo baskets. Keep in the fridge to set the mousse (about 30 minutes).

for the raspberry coulis

500 g/1 lb fresh raspberries

2 dspn caster sugar,
to taste

1 Heat the raspberries and caster sugar in a saucepan. Bring to the boil so the juices run, then immediately take off the heat. Stir well to make sure the sugar has all dissolved.

2 Allow to cool, then pass through a sieve (a conical sieve is the easiest). Place in the refrigerator to keep cool.

to serve

24 Cape gooseberries

to assemble the puddings

1 Open up the Cape gooseberries and remove a third of the 'paper lantern' so the fruit can be seen and sits better on the plate.

2 Spoon a small amount of raspberry coulis and rotate the plate so the coulis runs round and covers the plate.

3 Place a passion-fruit basket in the middle of each plate and decorate with one Cape gooseberry in each basket and three on each plate.

Tuile Baskets with Caramelized Apples, Mascarpone Cream and Raspberry Sauce

Colin and Duncan's Black Tie Dinner – Colin Beattie

serves eight

for the pastry

120 g/4 oz butter

120 g/4 oz plain flour

275 g/9 oz icing sugar

4 large egg whites

for the caramelized apples

5 large Granny Smith apples

juice of 1 lemon

175 g/6 oz butter

120 g/4 oz soft brown sugar +
a little extra

for the mascarpone cream

175 ml/6 fl oz double cream

250 g/8 oz Mascarpone cheese

for the raspberry sauce

500 g/1 lb raspberries

250 ml/8 fl oz port or
500 ml/16 fl oz of dessert wine

sugar to taste

to make the pastry

1 Preheat the oven to 180°C/350°F/Gas mark 4. Melt the butter and allow to cool.
2 Sift the flour and icing sugar into a bowl.
3 Whisk the egg whites until soft but not stiff.
4 Sift the flour and icing sugar into the egg whites; fold in with a metal spoon.
5 Add the cooled butter and fold in gently. The pastry should resemble a sticky cake batter.
6 Line baking sheets with baking parchment. Draw circular outlines on the parchment, two per sheet, using a small saucer as a template.
7 Spread the batter carefully with the blade of a flexible knife to fit the outlines. Lift on to the baking sheets and bake one at a time for 8–10 minutes.
8 Remove from the oven and mould while soft over a round shape (e.g. a satsuma) to form a basket; set aside.

to make the caramelized apples

1 Peel, core and slice the apples and pour over the lemon juice to prevent the slices from browning.
2 Melt the butter in a pan; add the sugar and the apples and cook until tender. Remove the fruit from the sugar and butter residue.
3 Cook the sugar and butter residue gently to evaporate the apple juices, until you have a thick, toffeeish, coating consistency. Add to the apples.

▶

to make the mascarpone cream

1 Make the mascarpone cream by combining the double cream and the mascarpone.

to make the raspberry sauce

1 Make the raspberry sauce by simmering all the ingredients together until the sauce reduces and thickens. Then pass through a sieve to remove the pips.

to assemble the desserts

1 Just before assembling the dish, add the extra sugar to the apples and use a blow torch, if you have one, to caramelize them. Or just sauté over a medium heat.

2 Assemble the dish by first putting a little of the mascarpone cream on the plate to hold the basket in place.

3 Put a spoonful of mascarpone cream in each basket, followed by the caramelized apples.

4 Finish off by surrounding each basket with a pool of raspberry sauce.

Iced Carrot Halva
Ayurvedic Christening Dinner – Shaila Parthasarathi

serves six

for the orange syrup

6–8 oranges

45 g/1½ oz granulated sugar

to make the orange syrup

1 Pare some zest from one of the oranges. Squeeze the juice from all the oranges; you will need about 6–8 oranges in total. Reserve a little orange juice. Heat the juice with the sugar and orange zest until reduced by half.

2 Soak the sultanas in the reserved orange juice for half an hour.

▶

for the cardamom cream

6–8 cardamom pods

150 ml/¼ pint crème fraîche

icing sugar

for the halva

25 g/1 oz golden sultanas

75 g/3 oz ghee (see method)

500 g/1 lb carrots, peeled and coarsely grated

450ml/¾ pint water

120 g/4 oz granulated sugar

50 g/2 oz blanched almonds, cut into slivers

50 g/2 oz pistachios, roughly chopped or crushed

seeds of 1 tspn cardamom pods, ground

150 ml/¼ pint crème fraîche

to make the cardamom cream

1 Remove the cardamom seeds from the pods and finely crush them. Fold into the crème fraîche with a little icing sugar, to taste.

to make the ghee

1 Make ghee by melting the butter in a small pan and heating it until the frothing stops and the butter begins to take on a brown colour. Remove from the heat and skim off any froth. Allow to cool for a couple of minutes. Then decant into a bowl, preferably through fine muslin, to ensure the burnt sediment remains separate. Discard the sediment.

to make the halva

1 Put the grated carrot in a saucepan and add the water. Bring to the boil, reduce the heat and simmer for 20–30 minutes, or until all the water is absorbed. The carrots should be soft but still separate.

2 Add the sugar and cook for a further 5 minutes. Allow to cool.

3 Drain and chop the sultanas. Add to the carrots, along with the ghee, almonds, pistachios, crushed cardamoms and crème fraîche.

4 Pack into six lightly greased dariole moulds and chill for at least 2 hours.

to serve

1 Pour some orange syrup on to each plate. Invert the moulds and place a halva in the middle of the puddle of orange syrup. Serve with a scoop of cardamom cream.

Chocolate Fondue with Fruit Kebabs

In the Search of Love – Simon Kelton

serves eight

for the fondue

175 g/6 oz hazelnuts

500 g/1 lb good-quality dark chocolate

600 ml/1 pint whipping cream

2 tbspn honey

2 tbspn Drambuie

for the fruit kebabs

500 g/1 lb strawberries, halved if large

fresh or tinned pineapple chunks

4 peaches, stoned and cut in chunks

8 apricots, stoned and halved

4 medium bananas, cut in 1 cm/½ in chunks

16–24 large seedless grapes

to make the fondue

1 Grind the hazelnuts until they are the size of coffee granules. Toast them in a dry frying-pan, under the grill or in a hot oven until lightly browned.

2 Chop the chocolate in a food processor until it forms granules.

3 Heat the cream until just scalded.

4 Place the fondue pot on the stove (or use the heaviest-bottomed pan or casserole you have), on a very gentle heat.

5 Place the chocolate in the fondue and melt it very gently and carefully: it will spoil if it gets too hot.

6 Slowly stir in the cream.

7 Stir in the hazelnuts, honey and Drambuie.

to make the kebabs

1 Thread a selection of fruit on each skewer.

2 Dip the fruit kebabs into the chocolate fondue.

Ron and Pam's Stuffed Pears

The West Essex Gourmet's Reunion – Ron Heath

serves eight

8 large Comice pears, with stalks intact

finely grated zest and juice of 2 lemons

caster sugar, for dredging

double cream, to serve

for the stuffing

120 g/4 oz unsalted butter

50 g/2 oz caster sugar

50 g/2 oz ground almonds

50 g/2 oz glacé cherries

grated zest of 2 lemons

pinch of ground cinnamon

1 dspn Kirsch

1 Preheat the oven to 160°C/325°F/Gas mark 3. Peel the pears, keeping the stalks intact. Brush each one with lemon juice, to prevent it from discolouring. Slice off the tops of the pears about 2.5 cm/1 in below the stalks.

2 Hollow out the centre of the pears with a scoop, discarding all the pips.

to make the stuffing

1 Beat together the butter and caster sugar. Stir in the ground almonds, glacé cherries, lemon zest, cinnamon and kirsch. This can be done a day or two in advance, if you like; keep in the fridge until needed.

2 Fill each pear with stuffing and replace the tops carefully.

3 Place each pear on a square of buttered foil. Pour over a little more lemon juice and dredge lightly with caster sugar. Draw up the foil loosely and twist it at the top around the stalk.

4 Place the pears on a baking tray and cook for about 45–50 minutes. Serve in the foil parcels, with cream.

Lime and Chilli Sorbet

The Chilli Boys – Eddie Baines and Steve Donovan

A sorbet that sounds hot but tastes refreshingly cool.

serves four

375 g/12 oz caster sugar

200 ml/7 fl oz water

grated zest of 4 limes

1 fresh, mild green chilli

1 fresh, mild red chilli

200 ml/7 fl oz lime juice
(approximately 12 limes)

1 egg white

1 Add the sugar to the water and stir over a low heat until it has dissolved. Bring to the boil and bubble rapidly for 5 minutes, to make a light syrup. Throw in the lime zest and leave to cool.

2 Meanwhile, seed the chillies and chop into very thin strips, about 1 cm/½ in long. Blanch in boiling water to remove the heat. Put in cold water. The heat should be almost gone; the chillies are more for colour and texture.

3 Stir the lime juice into the syrup. At this point you can add the chilli pieces and the egg white and pour the mixture into an ice-cream machine until frozen. Alternatively, use the traditional 'freeze and whisk' method. Do not add the chillies and egg white yet, but transfer the mixture into a mixing bowl and put in the freezer for about an hour, or until partially frozen. Remove from the freezer, and whisk the frozen bits back into the syrup. Replace in the freezer, allow to part-freeze once more, then remove and whisk again. Now the mixture should be thick and slushy.

4 Whisk the egg white to form soft peaks. Carefully fold into the partly frozen sorbet; then fold in the chilli pieces. Return to the freezer and leave until completely frozen. Remove from the freezer 30 minutes before serving, to soften.

Classic Puddings

Bread & Butter Pudding with Marmalade Sauce
All Over the Pacific – Penny Sinclair

serves six to eight

1½ sticks of stale French bread

good unsalted butter

1.75 litres/3 pints milk

24 cardamom pods

3 eggs

3 tbspn ground cinnamon

1 tbspn grated nutmeg

for the sauce

2 tbspn marmalade

1 tbspn Calvados

1   Slice the bread into 3cm/1½ in pieces. Liberally butter each piece on both sides. Put the pieces into a buttered baking dish.

2   In a pan, put 600 ml/1 pint of milk and 8 cardamom pods. Bring to the boil and scald. Strain and allow to cool.

3   Add 1 egg, 1 tbspn cinnamon and 1 tspn nutmeg to the milk. Beat the mixture well and pour over the bread and butter. Leave to soak until all the mixture has been absorbed.

4   Turn the bread over and repeat the process with some more scalded milk, egg and spices. When this has been absorbed, turn the bread over. Make a third amount of the milk, egg and spices mixture and pour it over (add a little cream at this stage, if you want a very rich pudding).

5   Preheat the oven to 200°C/400°F/Gas mark 6 and bake for approximately 45 minutes.

to make the sauce

1   Combine the marmalade and Calvados in a pan and warm gently. Take the bread and butter pudding out of the oven, spoon the marmalade and Calvados over it and serve.

Large Summer Pudding

Pukka Polo Picnic – Emma Sturt

You could also use loganberries, mulberries and redcurrants.

serves eight to ten

375 g/12 oz blackcurrants

120 g/4 oz white currants

375 g/12 oz cherries, stoned

250 g/8 oz sugar

sachet of gelatine

375 g/12 oz strawberries

250 g/8 oz bilberries

375 g/12 oz raspberries

large white sliced loaf

1 Poach the blackcurrants, white currants and cherries for 15 minutes, with a lid on, until softened.

2 Dissolve the sugar with 6 tbspn of water. Add the gelatine and stir well until it dissolves. Then add the blackcurrants, white currants, cherries, strawberries, bilberries and raspberries and cook, stirring gently for another 5 minutes.

3 Pour off about a third of the liquid from the saucepan into a shallow dish.

4 Take the crusts off the bread and cut to shape to line a large, flexible plastic pudding basin. Keep three or four slices for the top. Carefully dip the slices of bread into the liquid, one at a time, coating both sides to make them red.

5 Line the basin with a single layer of bread right up to the brim. Pour in half the fruit and then make another layer of bread in the middle. Add another layer of fruit. Reduce the rest of the liquid by half, to thicken. Pour on the remains of the juice until it covers the fruit. Place the last pieces of bread on top.

6 Put a plate over the top of the pudding basin to weigh it down. Chill for at least 4 hours.

7 Remove the plate and place a large plate upside-down over the basin. Invert and flex the sides of the bowl until the pudding loosens from the basin.

Rhubarb Rice Pudding

Wynne's Last Supper – Wynne Fearfield

Wynne's husband, Mike, said he loathed rice pudding. But Wynne has always loved it so, in an attempt to convert him, she consulted her cookbooks for three modern and delightful variations on the nursery food classic. I had to help her choose between them for her dinner and it wasn't easy. After happily guzzling all three, I plumped for the rhubarb version.

This recipe is adapted from **Rhodes Around Britain** *by Gary Rhodes.*

serves four–six

50 g/2 oz unsalted butter

500 g/1 lb rhubarb, cut in 3 cm/1½ in pieces

120 g/4 oz caster sugar

120 g/4 oz short-grain pudding rice

600 ml/1 pint milk

50 g/2 oz caster sugar

4 egg yolks

150 ml/¼ pint double cream

1 tspn per ramekin demerara or caster sugar

1 Heat the oven to 180°C/350°F/Gas mark 4.

2 Melt half the butter in a pan and add the rhubarb and the 120 g/4 oz caster sugar. Cook on a high heat for about 4 minutes. Stir occasionally but take care not to break up the rhubarb.

3 Drain the rhubarb through a sieve, reserving the juice, then spoon the rhubarb into ramekins, filling each one about half full.

4 Put the rice in a saucepan, cover with cold water and bring to the boil. Drain and rinse with cold water.

5 Bring to the boil three-quarters of the milk, 25 g/1 oz caster sugar and the rest of the butter in a pan.

6 Add the rice. Bring back to the boil and simmer for about 10 minutes, until the rice is *al dente*.

7 Beat the egg yolks and remaining sugar together. Boil the cream and remaining milk and pour on to the yolks, stirring. Mix with the rice and the reserved rhubarb juices.

8 Spread the rice mixture on top of the rhubarb, almost to the top of each ramekin.

9 Stand the ramekins in a baking tray filled with hot water and bake in the preheated oven for about 30 minutes, until the mixture is set but still slightly wobbly.

▶

10 Remove from the baking tray and leave to go completely cold. Chilling in the fridge will help to prevent the mixture from bubbling up.

11 To make a crème brûlée topping, sprinkle a thin, even layer of demerara or caster sugar over the top of each ramekin. Glaze with a blow torch or put under a very hot grill until the sugar is melted and lightly browned.

12 Serve hot or cold. For an alternative presentation, do not give the rice puddings a brûlée top or layer on top of drained rhubarb, but turn them out onto plates and serve surrounded by a sauce made from sieved rhubarb.

Clootie Dumpling

A Nice Bit of Brisket – Josie Livingstone

An old, clean pillowcase, cut in half and tied with string, makes a good dumpling bag.

serves a lot of people!

250 g/8 oz margarine
1 kg/2 lb/8 cups self-raising flour
150 g/5 oz/1½ cups sugar
4 tspns ground mixed spice
4 tspns ground cinnamon
1 kg/2 lb/8 cups dried fruit
4 dspn black treacle
4 dspn golden syrup
8 eggs, beaten
450 ml/¾ pint milk

1 Rub the fat into the flour. Stir in the sugar, mixed spice and cinnamon. The mixture should resemble breadcrumbs.

2 Make a well, add the dried fruit and pour in the treacle, syrup, eggs and milk. Stir and mix together well.

3 Soak a linen or cotton 'dumpling bag' under the cold tap and wring out. Smooth out and put the mixture into the centre. Tie up tightly.

4 Into a very large pan of water, lower a heatproof plate. Bring the water to the boil and put in the dumpling bag. Boil for 4 hours (the plate will rattle – if it stops, the water's gone off the boil).

Pozzi's Pavlova

Pozzi's Pavlova – Marion Postma

serves four greedy old ladies!

10 egg whites

500 g/1 lb caster sugar

for the filling

600ml/1 pint double cream

500 g/1 lb fresh raspberries

1 Preheat the oven to 140°C/275°F/Gas Mark 1. Line two baking sheets with greaseproof paper.

2 Place all the egg whites in a large mixing bowl and whisk until they form soft peaks. Gradually add the caster sugar, being careful not to over-beat the eggs.

3 Using your hands, scoop out the mixture, dividing it equally between the two baking sheets. Form them both into circles about 25 cm/10 in in diameter and 5 cm/2 in high. Bake for 5–6 hours.

4 When completely cool, whip the cream and cover one of the meringues with a thick layer. Then add a generous layer of raspberries. Place the second meringue on top to form a sandwich.

5 Put the rest of the cream into a piping bag and carefully pipe decorative rosettes on to the top layer. Decorate these with individual raspberries and serve.

Pannacotta

Greco-Italian Surprise Party – Marina Schofield

serves twenty

1½ sachets of gelatine

1 tbspn milk

1 litre/2½ pints single cream

250 g/8 oz sugar

1 vanilla pod

for the caramel topping

175 g/6 oz sugar

250 ml/8 fl oz water

1 Empty the sachets of gelatine into a microwave-proof bowl. Add a little milk. Leave to go spongy.

2 To make the syrup topping: in another saucepan, put the sugar and water and reduce until a very dark brown, bubbling syrup is formed.

3 Pour the syrup on to the bottom of a 1.75-litre (3-pint) dish. Gently swirl the caramelizing syrup around the bowl, so the syrup adheres about 2 cm/¾ in up the sides. Leave to harden.

4 In a large saucepan, put the cream, sugar and vanilla pod and bring to a very gentle slow boil; then turn the heat down to a gentle simmer and keep stirring.

5 Meanwhile, put the gelatine in the microwave for 45 seconds at High. The mixture should melt and become runny.

6 Add the gelatine milk mixture to the cream mixture. Stir in and remove from the heat. Remove the vanilla pod and pour the cream mixture on top of the hardened caramel syrup. Leave to set in the fridge overnight.

Zabaglione

Raising the Roof, Italian Style – Teresa Ibbotsen

serves eight

16 egg yolks

8 dspn caster sugar

175 ml/6 fl oz Marsala

1 In a large metal bowl, mix the egg yolks and sugar. Beat with an electric whisk or hand whisk until the mixture is pale and creamy.

2 After about 4 minutes, start adding the Marsala, a little at a time.

3 Once all the Marsala has been added, place the bowl over a pan of simmering water and continue to whisk for a further 15–20 minutes. Don't let the water boil too fast, otherwise the mixture will curdle. Once the mixture has thickened, pour into warmed wine glasses and serve straight away.

Tarte Tatin

Tory Blues – Marguerite Vincent

serves six to eight

for the rich shortcrust pastry

250 g/8 oz plain flour

150 g/5 oz butter

75 g/3 oz icing sugar

1 egg yolk

2 tbspn cold water

for the filling

500 g/1 lb prepared fruit, e.g. apples or pears

2 tbspn brown sugar

1 Make the pastry by sifting the flour into a bowl; rub in the butter. Stir in the icing sugar and mix in the egg yolk. Add the water, drop by drop – the amount given may be too much in some cases. Roll into a ball and chill in the fridge for at least 30 minutes.

2 Preheat the oven to 200°C/400°F/Gas mark 6. Grease the surface of your large non-stick or pottery dish thickly with butter and sprinkle it with the brown sugar. Lay the fruit on top, cut-side up, in neat rows.

3 Roll out the pastry to the size of the dish and cover the fruit.

4 Cook the tart for 30–45 minutes.

5 Leave to cool for a few minutes. Place your serving dish over the pastry and carefully turn upside-down, so that the fruit is now on top.

'Boiled Baby'

Gorse Warrior's Barn Feast – Pigeon Biter

Why is it that so many suet puddings have 'naughty nicknames' – Spotted Dick, Matron's Bosom, etc? Pigeon theorised, credibility, that they were staples in the forces and got their alternative sobriquets from waggish soldiers and sailors. You can see what they were thinking of here. Plump and smug in its cotton cloth, the resemblance to a tightly wrapped neonate is plain to see.

serves ten

625 g/1¼ lb mixed dried fruit

cider

50 g/2 oz sugar

1 tspn ground ginger

500 g/1 lb self-raising flour, sifted

1 tspn salt

250 g/8 oz suet

to serve

molasses

clotted cream

1. Soak the fruit in enough cider to cover for a few hours or, preferably, overnight.
2. Drain the fruit thoroughly and add the sugar and ginger.
3. Mix the flour with the salt and suet. Make a well in the centre and, with a knife, mix enough cold water to form a dough that doesn't stick to the sides of the bowl. Flour your surface well.
4. Roll out the pastry in a rectangle a 5 mm/¼ in thick, with the widest side closest to you.
5. Spread an even layer of fruit over the pastry, leaving 5 cm/2 in at the sides. Fold over the end closest to you, tuck in either side and gently roll away from you.
6. Wrap the 'baby' in a clean muslin or cotton cloth, tie with string at both ends and place in boiling water in a large pan or fish kettle. Cook for 4 hours, turning once during cooking.
7. Serve with molasses and clotted cream.

Tiramisu

Old Girls' Reunion – Heather Matuozzo

serves eight to ten

1 cup strong coffee

4 tbspn Amaretto liqueur

500 g/1 lb mascarpone cheese

60 g/2 oz drinking chocolate powder

600 ml/1 pint custard, cooled

for the sponge

250 g/8 oz self-raising flour

250 g/8 oz sugar

250 g/8 oz soft margarine

2 tspn baking powder

4 eggs

to decorate

4 Amaretti biscuits, crushed

handful of 'hundreds and thousands'

1 Preheat the oven to 200°C/400°F/Gas mark 6. Put all the sponge ingredients in a bowl and beat together. Pour into a greased, 25 x 18 cm/10 x 6 in, rectangular baking tin or ovenproof dish. Bake for half an hour.

2 When cool, cut into fingers. Pour the coffee and amaretto into a bowl and mix well. Have another large bowl ready. Dip the sponge fingers quickly in the liquid and layer in the bottom of the large bowl.

3 Spread a layer of mascarpone on top, sprinkle with chocolate powder and repeat the layering process until you are 2.5 cm/1 in from the top of the bowl. Make the custard and pour it on top of the last layer. Put in the fridge to set.

4 Sprinkle with crushed Amaretti biscuits and 'hundred and thousands' and serve.

Open-fire Sponge Pudding

Teepee Tea – Sam Thornley

You might have thought that an open fire places severe limitations on the repertoire of a cook and that puddings would suffer in particular. But Sam Tharnley proved, in his teepee, that with a little ingenuity nothing's impossible. This dish was a great triumph.

serves six to eight

1 large organic Bramley apple

5 organic Victoria plums

1 tbspn organic honey

1 tbspn apple juice

75 g/3 oz hazelnuts in shells

75 g/3 oz vegetable suet

175 g/6 oz self-raising flour

75 g/3 oz raisins

1 free-range egg

1 tbspn milk

75 g/3 oz brown sugar, to decorate

1 Lightly stew the apples and plums with the honey and some apple juice for liquid.

2 Shell, roast or toast and crush the hazelnuts.

3 Mix the dry ingredients and then beat in the egg and enough milk to produce a 'dollopy' texture. Dollop on top of the stewed fruit in an ovenproof dish and cover with the lid. Cook for at least an hour, in a cast-iron pan suspended over the fire on chitties. The liquid in the fruit will steam the suet mixture and make it puff up. Alternatively, bake, covered, in the oven, at 180°C/350°F/Gas mark 4, for an hour.

4 When the top is cooked, take the cast-iron pan lid and heat it until scorching in the fire. Sprinkle brown sugar on the top of the pudding and then sear with the hot lid, so that the top caramelizes and browns.

The Cooks

Gordon's Table – Gordon Perrier
Gilded Pears with Goat's Cheese 56
Mango Fool 151

Valencian Paella Party – Dave Hayward
Tomato Bread with Spanish Ham 14
Anchovy and Black Olive Toasts 15
Valencian Paella 112

The Chilli Boys – Eddie Baines and Steve Donovan
Grilled Shark Steaks, Marinated in Lime with Mole Sauce 68
Refried Beans 132
Lime and Chilli Sorbet 167

Wynne's Last Supper – Wynne Fearfield
Braised Oxtail with Celeriac 80
Wynne's Super Creamy Mashed Potatoes 137
Rhubarb Rice Pudding 170

A Futurist Feast – Celia Lyttleton
Italian Flag 13
Bandaged Fish 65
Italian Breasts in Sunshine 154

Yorkshire Sunday Best – Stewart Ibbotson
Italian-style Roast Potatoes 128
Yorkshire Pudding with Sage, Shallots and Sweet Onion Gravy 130

The French Connection – Selina Snow
Sea Bass baked with Fennel, Lemon and Thyme with Saffron and Lemon
    Mayonnaise 72
Prune and Armagnac Tart 146

Rumble in the Jungle – Felicity Keebaugh
Chicken and Lemongrass Soup 20
Squid with Noodles and Vegetable Tentacles 66
Rambutan Ice Cream 159

Late Starter – Wendy Ingham
Onion and Goat's Cheese Tarts with Walnut Pastry 59
Chicken with Tarragon 99
Gratin Dauphinois 134
Chocolate and Coffee Mousse cakes 144

Gourmet Night – Gordon Irvine
Quails' Eggs in Smoked Salmon Nests with Lime Mayonnaise 30
Haunch of Wild Boar Roasted with Herbs and Garlic, in a Red-Wine Sauce 82
Calvados Sorbet 156
Passion-fruit Mousse in Filo Baskets with a Raspberry Coulis and Cape
     Gooseberries 160

**Caribbean Birthday Surprise – Trisha Wallace
and Alison Haughton**
Saltfish and Ackee Vol-au-vents 16
Fried Plantains 133
Rice and Peas 129
Pat's Coconut Pie 142

The Karahi Club – Nina and Sumita Dhand
Murgh Makhani 102
Bhurta (Aubergine Masala) 135

Tea for the Girls – Enid Jean
Paté Tartlets 18

Reg's Front Room Bistro – Reg Gray
Gigot d'agneau Cuit dans le Foin (Lamb in Hay) 89

Seventies Night – Monica Curtain and Sue Smallwood
Sweet Baby Soul Burgers with Hot Corn Relish 124

Tuscany-by-Doncaster – Michael Masserella
Grilled Polenta with Wild Mushrooms and Red Onions 60
Sweet White Wine Granita with Mixed Berries 153

The Boys Shoot – Anthony Zahara
Casseroled Pheasant with Kumquats 101

Christmas Tree - Tony Kitchell
Goose Kebabs, with Cranberry and Port Sauce 104
Chestnut Kebabs 127

Leaving Liverpool – Jon Ashton
Black Pudding Wontons with Balsamic Sauce 41
Vegetable Tower Provencal 123
Pecan Pie 149

Tory Blues – Marguerite Vincent
Pissaladière Canapés 17
Raised Pie 88
Tarte Tatin 174

Mushroom Magic – Bob Wootton
Terrine of Sweetbreads with Morels 46
Beef with Ceps 87

Chinese Moon Festival – Rose Billaud
Squid stuffed with Minced Pork, Shrimps and Mushrooms 75
Sweet and Sour Pork 86
Duck with Lily Flowers and Chinese Mushrooms 105

Trafalgar Night Fever – Holly Waghorn
Saucy Spratlings with a Spicy Split-pea Sauce 36

Pozzi's Pavlova – Marion Postma
Beef Wellington 96
Pozzi's Pavlova 172

Old Girls' Reunion – Heather Matuozzo
Minestrone Madras with Spicy Bruschetta 22
Curried Cannelloni 121
Tiramisu 176

Welcome to the World – Sue O'Neil
Koulibiac 37
Rosie's Placenta Pâté 45

Run Rabbit Run – Hilary Waterhouse
Pigeon Pâté with Flowerpot Bread 42
Rabbit Casserole 107

Ayurvedic Christening Dinner – Shaila Parthasarathi
Iced Carrot Halva 163

The Policeman's Ball – Paul Francey
Gin and Tonic Sorbet 155

Greco-Italian Surprise Party – Marina Schofield
Taramasalata 29
Moussaka 85
Pannacotta 173

The Feast of Samhain – Ozi Osmond
Cockles and Laverbread 33
Rack of Pork 91

Keeping up Appearances – June Ainsworth
Puff Pastries with Anchovy Ice Cream 31

The Laird's Supper – Michael Dudgeon
Highland Pibroch 39
Venison Glen Loth 108

The West Essex Gourmets' Reunion – Ron Heath
Lobster Pâté with Rosé Sauce 32
Ron and Pam's Stuffed Pears 166

Teen Girls Sleepover – Leah Scott
Leah's Lasagne 117

Gumbo Loft Party – Brenlen Jinkens
Stuffed Crabs 76
Gumbo 71

Ancient Greek Symposium – Dimitris Vassilliou
Seared Tuna 73
Squid stuffed with Fetta Cheese and Mushrooms 64
Roast Kid 93

In Search of Love – Simon Kelton
Gravadlax with Dill and Mustard Mayonnaise 38
Snipe and Woodcock à la Gourmande 106
Chocolate Fondue with Fruit Kebabs 165

Raising the Roof, Italian Style – Teresa Ibbotsen
Sugo 94
Spinach and Ricotta Ravioli 118
Zabaglione 174

A Vegan Theatre Picnic – Rachel Markham
Vegetable Terrine 58
Chocolate Orange Pots 152

Trawlerman's Supper – George Dyer
Seafood Fishcakes with Garlic and Chilli Sauce 34
Turbot Liver Pâté 29
Whole John Dory in Red Wine Sauce 67

Pukka Polo Picnic – Emma Sturt
Coronation Chicken 44
'Salmon in the Sink' 70
Large Summer Pudding 169

Gorse Warrior's Barn Feast – Pigeon Biter
Marinated and Barbecued Lamb 97
Hare and Venison Pie 98
'Boiled Baby' 175

Scouts Honour – Niamh Watmore
Corn, Chilli and Cheese Soup 23
Chicken Fajitas with Tortillas 110
Amaretti Chocolate Torte 147

A Jamaican Farewell – Paige Mulroy
Nettle Soup 27
Baked Jerk Duck 109
Sweet Potato Pudding 145

First House-warming Vietnam-Style – Thi Nguyen
Summer Rolls 52
Whelks stuffed with Minced Pork 77

A Kosher Celebration – Lindsey Jacobs
Chicken Soup with Kneidlich and Lockshen 26

Index